CELTIC SOCCER CREW

JOHN O'KANE

CELTIC SOCCER CREW

WHAT THE HELL DO WE CARE

JB

JOHN BLAKE

Published by John Blake Publishing Ltd,
3 Bramber Court, 2 Bramber Road,
London W14 9PB, England

www.johnblakepublishing.co.uk

www.facebook.com/Johnblakepub   facebook

twitter.com/johnblakepub   twitter

First published by Pennant Books in 2006.
This edition published in paperback in 2012

ISBN: 978-1-84358-958-7

British Library Cataloguing-in-Publication Data:

A catalogue record for this book is available from the British Library.

Design by www.envydesign.co.uk

Printed in Great Britain by CPI Group (UK) Ltd, Croydon, CR0 4YY

1 3 5 7 9 10 8 6 4 2

Papers used by John Blake Publishing are natural, recyclable products
made from wood grown in sustainable forests. The manufacturing
processes conform to the environmental regulations of the
country of origin.

Every attempt has been made to contact the relevant copyright-holders,
but some were unobtainable. We would be grateful if the
appropriate people could contact us.

ACKNOWLEDGEMENTS

Thanks to the Jacobite and the Elgin bhoys, Wee Eck and Allan T, Jambo, Paul, John McG, Galtee bhoy, Fast Ed, Fraser, drummer bhoy, Wee Tam and all the lads in the CSC... Special thanks to all at Pennant Books.

PROLOGUE

This book is an honest account of football violence and how it has affected my life and the lives of those around me. I will not attempt to glorify or condone the life that I and hundreds of others choose to live. What I hope to achieve by writing this book is to give an honest and candid portrayal of life as a football hooligan from the point of view of my own real life experiences.

I am sick and tired of middle-class academics who believe that they are in a position to comment on the worldwide phenomenon that is football violence. These social workers, politicians and psychologists are the same people who go on 'team-building' courses that include white-water rafting, paintball war games and any number of other extreme sports, yet they still feel the need to condemn football hooligans.

In my view, they are boring, lonely people who are searching for that adrenalin rush and excitement that their safe, uneventful lives are lacking. However hard they try, they will never experience what we get time after time from a good battle at the football. For the purposes of this book, and for fairly obvious reasons, I have changed some of the names and will leave out some events in order to protect the guilty. The people that were involved know who they are and therefore don't need to see their names in print. Those who asked in advance for a mention will be deliberately left out, as they are most likely the bottle-throwers and window-smashers who never went toe-to-toe in their lives.

My memory may be a little rusty (probably as a result of the amount of blows taken to the head!). Throughout this book, however, I have tried to give as truthful an account as possible of the triumphs, beatings and scams that I have been involved in.

CHAPTER 1

There is nothing unusual about the way my parents met; my dad, Andy, was a bus driver with the Glasgow Corporation, while my mother worked in the same depot as a conductress. Romance blossomed and they courted for a while before announcing their engagement. This created a stir amongst both families, who voiced their concerns and misgivings. The reason for the commotion was the fact my mother came from a staunch Scottish Protestant family, while my dad was born to Irish parents who had moved from Derry to Glasgow when he was about 10. This was 1960s Glasgow, a city divided by sectarian bigotry and religious intolerance, where mixed marriages, although not unheard of, were frowned upon.

Despite all their problems, my parents went ahead with their marriage in 1962. The newlyweds set up home on the council estate of Castlemilk, which at the time was regarded as a modern and innovative estate which boasted such luxuries as inside toilets, with hot and cold running water in the bathroom. The reality was, Castlemilk was a sprawling neighbourhood, perched on the southernmost tip of the city boundary, which lacked the basic amenities such as shops and banks, and didn't have a pub up until the early 1980s. Despite the apparent oversight by the city planners, families flocked to Castlemilk, often from the slum tenements that had been earmarked for demolition in places like the Gorbals.

Not long after settling in Castlemilk, my dad gave up his job as a bus driver to take up a well-paid job as an engineer in the massive Hoover factory in nearby Cambuslang. My mum then gave up work after falling pregnant with my elder sister, Anne, who was born in February 1964. I am the youngest of three, born amazingly the same year as my brother, Andrew, who was born in February 1968 while I was born 10 days before Christmas.

It is hard to imagine how my mother coped with two babies and a four-year-old all demanding her attention. She also had to attend to the usual demands of the Christmas and New Year festivities. Things were tough, but my mum and dad managed without any major crises in the first year after I was born. However, the last thing my mum needed was a visit from the police on 3 January 1970. They had called to inform her about my dad having been arrested at the Old Firm game that day. My dad was an avid Celtic fan and had gone to the traditional Old Firm New Year's derby which was at Celtic Park that day. The policeman said my dad had been arrested along with his friend and was being held on a charge of breach of the peace for allegedly throwing a bottle at Rangers fans.

In those days, Celtic Park was one of the largest stadiums in Europe, frequently housing crowds of up to 90,000. The stadium consisted of a grandstand with sloping terraces behind each goal and was completed by the famous Jungle, which was a roofed enclosure that ran the length of the pitch opposite the grandstand. Back in the 60s, both Rangers and Celtic fans occupied the Jungle, separated only by a small wall and a thin line of police officers. This was also the time that supporters were allowed to take their own alcohol into the stadium, which usually resulted in them tossing their empties at the opposing fans, sometimes having first pissed in them. My mother was informed by the policeman that my dad and his mate were to remain in custody until the courts resumed following the festive break.

They eventually appeared at Central Glasgow Magistrates' Court, whereupon they pleaded guilty and received a substantial fine. However, their relief at getting fined was short-lived, as the magistrate announced that he was not prepared to allow my dad and his mate any time to pay the fine, which meant they were sent to the notorious Barlinnie Prison until such time that their family or friends could raise the money to pay the fines. My mum never tired of reminding me of how she struggled on and off buses and through the snow with three young children on her way to visit my dad in Barlinnie.

I think my dad and his mate spent a couple of nights in jail before the necessary amount was paid. I was obviously too young to remember anything about my first visit to Barlinnie, but unfortunately for me it would become an all-too-familiar place in later years.

We lived in Castlemilk until I was four, when, after a fire had gutted our house, my parents decided to move to Pollok, which was a similar housing estate on the south-west of Glasgow. Shortly after moving, my parents split up. I never got to hear the full story behind the split, but I do know that my dad didn't really want to move to Pollok as it was about 10 miles from his work, which was on the other side of the city.

The months that followed my dad's departure were particularly hard and saw my mum finding comfort with alcohol. I was by now at the same school as my brother and sister, which was St Monica's RC Primary School, one of the largest primaries in Glasgow. I enjoyed primary school and made it into the football team where I played in goal.

Home life was chaotic by the time I had reached Primary Year 7. My brother and sister were now at secondary school, while I was alone at St Monica's. To make matters worse for me, my brother had begun to take an interest in becoming a Jehovah's Witness, while my sister started to attend Rangers games. She even went to Hampden for the Scottish Cup Final in 1980, which Celtic won 1–0 after extra-time, which triggered a pitch invasion by jubilant Celtic fans. The Rangers fans reacted by joining their victorious rivals on the pitch, sparking the worst riot ever seen in Scottish football. My sister was on the pitch wearing a Rangers scarf. She claimed later that she wasn't aware of what was happening and had simply followed those around her.

Meanwhile, my mother was virtually bed-ridden. She had been knocked down by a hit-and-run driver, breaking her hip in the process. This created a lot of tension in the house, particularly between me and my mother. As a child, I suffered from various ailments that required medical attention, meaning numerous visits to hospital. My mum was now drinking daily and would, more often than not, be in no fit state to take me to my appointments.

Events eventually came to a head one day. I was due to attend another hospital appointment and, in an effort to ensure my mum wouldn't be too drunk to take me, I took the drink from her bedside cabinet when I thought she was asleep, and began to pour it down the toilet. My mum must have heard me when I was in her room because, as I was pouring the contents of her last can of lager down the toilet, she came barging into the toilet with her walking stick raised above her head. I was trying to stand up from the kneeling position I was in at the toilet pan, but before I made it to my feet the first of several blows landed on my body. I was in a panic and knew I had to escape before I suffered a severe beating. It wasn't the first time my mum had used her walking stick to hit me. I had required hospital treatment on one of the occasions, but there was something more sinister this time. There was nobody else in the house to stop my mum. I decided the only option was to climb out of the toilet window and into the porch at the front door.

I scrambled over the cistern, breaking some toiletries in the process as I escaped through the window. I had managed to get into the porch just as my mum opened the front door brandishing the walking stick. I made a dash for the open door behind her, knowing that I would probably be hit by the stick again, but also knowing that if I got into the house and locked my mum out I would be safe. I managed to get past my mum and slumped to the floor as the door slammed behind me, locking my mum out. She was banging furiously on the door for a while, before all of a sudden it went deathly silent. I didn't know what to think. I was terrified and in a great deal of pain as a result of the blows to my body.

It seemed like an age had passed when suddenly there was a chap at the door. I got up rather gingerly and looked through the spyhole, where I saw one of our neighbours. He asked me to let him in, assuring me that I would not be hit again. I was apprehensive, but believed I would be OK as my mum wouldn't dare hit me when there were witnesses there. I opened the door slowly, not knowing what to expect, when all of a sudden there was a push at the door so forceful it knocked me to the floor. The next thing I knew I was being pinned to the ground by two uniformed policemen. I was face down with my arms twisted up my back before the policemen put handcuffs on me. I was screaming and shouting for my mum to tell the police to leave me alone. However, all I got was a couple of knees in my back, which the police later referred to as 'restraining techniques'.

I was then dragged out of the house, down two flights of stairs and thrown into the back of a police van. I was taken to Pollok Police Station where the cuffs were taken off before I was put into a detention room. I couldn't understand what was happening; I was only 11 years of age and had never been in any sort of trouble before. I wasn't in the room for long before the door was opened and a policeman entered with a couple of social workers. One of the social workers I knew, as he had been involved with my family for the couple of months leading up to this incident. He explained to me that my mum had accused me of being out of her control and that I would be taken to appear at a Children's Panel to decide what was the best course of action for the social workers to adopt in dealing with this situation. The Children's Panel system is similar to juvenile courts and has the power to put children into care.

I was led out of the police station, placed into a black car and taken to an office building in the city centre where the Children's Panel hearing would be held. I was confused, feeling very alone and bewildered by the speed at which things were moving. I appeared in front of the panel, where the social worker gave an account of the events that led to me being taken from the house by the police. It transpired that my mum had accused me of refusing to go to school and smashing up the house before creating a siege situation. I was given an opportunity to explain my version of events, and I strongly denied the allegations made by my mother.

The panel decided that I would have to attend a hearing at the Sheriff Court because of the differences in my account compared to that of my mother. They told me that I would be placed in Larchgrove Assessment Centre for a period of three weeks. I was then put back into the black car and driven to Larchgrove. On arrival, I was taken into an office along with my social worker where I met the manager of the centre, who explained the day-to-day routine and then gave me a tour of the premises and its facilities. Larchgrove was originally a Borstal for young offenders. It was now an assessment centre for young people with a wide range of problems, ranging from boys accused of serious crimes including murder to youngsters like me who were experiencing problems at home. It was very intimidating. Here I was, a young boy who had never been in any trouble, mixing with serious young criminals, many of them who abused solvents such as glue and gas.

After a few days, when I had settled in, I was taken to the education department for school classes. I couldn't believe the work I was given to complete. I had recently started secondary school, but here I was being expected to carry out school work that was designed for Primary Year 3 or 4 children. I think the centre treated all the boys as illiterate delinquents. I pointed out to the school teacher that I wasn't happy with the lessons, prompting her to contact my school, who sent in appropriate work. Meanwhile, my three-week period had passed and I was no nearer to knowing where I would end up. This was due to the Children's Court hearing where the judge had dropped three of the allegations my mum had made against me, having chosen to believe my version of events. Eventually, after three months, it was decided I would be going to a children's home. This was a relief, as the alternative was a List O school, which is basically an approved school.

It was on my 12th birthday – so something you never forget – that I moved into Ganavan Children's Home, which is a big Victorian mansion in the affluent Pollokshields area of Glasgow. The children's home was a new life for me. I got new clothes and pocket money, and I was allowed to go to the football most weeks; all things that I rarely got in my mum's house. I think my mother, and more so my brother Andrew, resented this because when I went on home visits I always had money or new clothes, whereas he was still dressed in hand-me-downs. I also returned to my secondary school, Lourdes, which was in Cardonald, a couple of miles from Pollokshields.

My brother was in the year above me at Lourdes, and his becoming a committed Jehovah's Witness presented me with a few problems. Andrew was being ridiculed and having things thrown at him, and was basically a target for the bullies, but he wouldn't react at all so the bullies decided to turn their attention to me. I reacted the only way I know how, by taking the bullies on. The first year or two in school I was constantly fighting, but I was beginning to win more than I lost and soon the bullies turned their attention to other people, knowing they wouldn't get beaten up by them.

After a couple of years in Ganavan, I was moved to another home, Park Lodge, where I met my first girlfriend, Rita, who I went out with for about three years. I was 15 and doing very well at school, where I was in the football team, playing in goal. My grades were also quite good and I sat seven O levels, receiving Pass marks in five of them. Because of my birthday falling in December, I was required to stay on at school until my 16th birthday, which meant I had to go into the fifth year. I was planning to complete the full year and was studying hard for my Highers.

Then I received news that to this day I find hard to understand. The social workers in their wisdom decided I was to move out of the home and into my own tenancy shortly after my 16th birthday. This meant I had to leave school, as I couldn't continue with my education once I was in my house. This decision really annoyed me, and still does, because it denied me the opportunity to gain more qualifications. The obstacle which prevented me continuing at school was the benefit system at the time, which didn't make provisions for young householders who were also at school, meaning I had to sign on as unemployed in order to receive housing benefits.

I moved into my house in March 1985. It was located on the ground floor of a typical 1950s-built council tenement. I thought I would be able to cope on my own, but expected some support from the Social Work Department, if I needed it. However, my social worker moved to another post out of Pollok shortly after I had moved into my house. I wasn't allocated a new social worker or any other type of support and was basically left to fend for myself. It wasn't long before my house resembled a gang hut with my mates appearing most nights, drinking and playing cards into the small hours. Most of my mates were in the newly formed Pollok Bushwhackers which was the result of the amalgamation of two gangs, the Krew and the Kross. The majority of the lads in the Bushwhackers were also members of the Celtic Soccer Crew and adopted the name after some of us had gone to a Carlisle v Millwall match where we saw the infamous Millwall Bushwhackers. Gang fighting in this part of Glasgow was rife, with the Bushwhackers playing a very active part.

This could have cost me my life one night when, following a fight with a local gang in which one of the rivals got slashed, I was attacked in my own house. After the fight, a few lads came back to my house for a drink, before leaving at about midnight. I was preparing to go to bed when I was aware of a noise at the door. Thinking it was one of my mates who had forgotten something, I went to investigate. I was just about to open the door when all of a sudden it came flying off its hinges, knocking me to the floor. There was a group of about six strangers, all armed with long knives and baseball bats, lashing out in my direction. Fortunately for me, the door was on top of me, providing me with some protection. I can't say how long the attack lasted, but I consider myself to have been a very lucky man that night. One of my neighbours must have phoned the police, who arrived to find me sprawled on the floor.

I was taken to hospital where I received stitches, mostly to my arms and to where I had been stabbed through my top lip. The police had waited for me to be treated in the A&E Department and were expecting me to make a statement once I had been attended to. I told them I couldn't recall anything about the attack and didn't know of any motives. The police offered me a lift home, probably expecting me to offer more information, which I never gave them. I told them to take me to my mother's, as I didn't fancy returning to my own house. I was shocked when, after tapping at my mother's door, I was met with a barrage of abuse and refused entry. I didn't know where to go; it was after 2am. In desperation, I called my dad who, without any hesitation, told me to get a taxi to his house which he would pay for at the other end. My dad lived in Castlemilk, having returned there following the divorce from my mum. I hadn't had much contact with my dad and had only begun to see him on a regular basis after I had left the home.

I arrived at my dad's where I was welcomed with open arms. He had a spare room with a camp bed made up for me. Once in bed, I couldn't sleep. I was tossing and turning and thinking about all the stupid things that I had got myself involved in over the past year or so. My dad didn't know about my involvement with the Crew, which had begun about a year before I'd moved in with him.

CHAPTER 2

It was near the end of 1984 and just about every other team in Scotland seemed to have a Casual following. Aberdeen and Motherwell would come mob-handed to Celtic Park and run amok. There were pockets of Celtic fans who would offer some resistance, but it was unorganised and consisted of small groups from different housing schemes in Glasgow who were probably more interested in fighting each other.

I was part of a group that went to all the games. We originated from children's homes and the tough housing scheme of Pollok. We were all wannabe Casuals and up for a fight but we lacked organisation and numbers. This was all to change – mostly due to a chance encounter with Aberdeen one afternoon in Glasgow.

CELTIC SOCCER CREW

A crowd of us had arranged to meet in an amusement arcade in the city centre, under the bridge at Central Station. We were too young to meet at a pub as most of us ranged from about 14 to 17. We were milling about when we became aware of a group of Aberdeen Casuals heading towards the bridge from Buchanan Street. There were a couple of hundred of them, distinctive in their smart Pringle jumpers and red ski hats with the bobbles ripped from them.

The younger ones came into the amusement arcade, swaggering about and looking for trouble. There were about 15 of us at this time and we were all up for a fight. Some jostling and then a number of skirmishes broke out and quickly spilled into the street. Even though we were outnumbered, we stood our ground and I remember going toe-to-toe with one guy in particular. He was a wee stocky guy with specs wearing a Burberry jacket. As we were exchanging punches, more Aberdeen appeared from the pub. They chased us to the Hope Street end of the bridge. We had a bit of luck as there was a skip lying there that contained an array of weapons. We armed ourselves with poles and bars and ran towards Aberdeen. They were taken by surprise but stood their ground. A running battle followed, but didn't last long, as the police arrived quickly on the scene. Aberdeen, to their credit, also had a go at the cops. This deflected attention away from us and provided the opportunity for us to escape without any nickings.

This was my first taste of football violence and I suppose it must compare with a junkie taking his first hit – the high was unbelievable! The difference with me, however, was now I was truly hooked. I would go on to experience the same level of high on many more occasions over the years, unlike the addicts who go chasing their first hit forever.

When we got to the game, we couldn't stop talking about the fight we'd just had. We even decided to leave the match 10 minutes from time to go to the London Road end and wait for Aberdeen on their way out. We had a mob of about 20–30 looking for a fight. This ranged from mods, punks and wannabe Casuals to a few veterans of the boot-boy era. We didn't see ourselves as an organised mob – just a crowd of people who were up for a battle!

The coppers controlled the crowd outside without giving us any chance of a fight. They escorted Aberdeen down London Road and shepherded us on to a bus. Due to the after-match traffic, the bus took ages to get along the road, allowing Aberdeen, who were walking, to get ahead of us. We were approaching Bridgeton Cross when a group of Aberdeen, who looked like they had slipped their escort, started to taunt the Celtic supporters on the bus. The bus was packed with all sorts of Celtic fans and at first they just sang loudly and banged the windows; then, all of a sudden, someone standing close to me swung himself up using the handrail and booted a window out. It didn't take long until just about every window on the bus had been booted out and everyone was clambering out of the bus using exits they had just made for themselves. I think Aberdeen got a shock when they realised that this wasn't just another crowd of booze-filled scarfers, but a mob that was up for a battle.

However, they were more experienced in this type of fight, whereas we fought mostly as individuals. The police were again on the scene quickly and soon had things under control. That may have been the end of that particular fight, but it was the beginning of something much bigger. Like the helpless junkie, I had experienced this high and I craved my next hit.

The next few weeks were to see the launch of the Roman Catholic Casuals. Celtic had drawn Hamilton in some Cup competition and we had to travel to Douglas Park for the midweek fixture. A crowd of about 15 of us met on the train with other lads who had heard about the fracas with Aberdeen. We decided that it was time to get our act together with this amount of people interested. We agreed to meet at Central Station the following Saturday for the trip to Paisley, where Celtic were playing St Mirren.

The night before the game, I could hardly sleep for thinking about the forthcoming day. Silly things went through my mind, like what I would wear, who else would turn up, and trying to think of a name we could call ourselves. The Friday before the game, I had spent all my Post Office savings on a Tacchini tracksuit and a pair of Adidas Trim Trab trainers. I even got my hair cut into a wedge with an inch line. I thought I was the bees-knees!

We had arranged to meet at about one o'clock in the station. Our crowd consisted of the usual 15 plus a couple of new recruits, all resplendent in our new tracksuits and Pringles. When we got to the station concourse, we noticed small groups of lads milling about. It was as if there was an air of uncertainty and a lack of leadership. We recognised a few faces among each of the groups, and called them over, where they each introduced themselves. We travelled through to Paisley with a mob of 70 for our first game together as Celtic Casuals.

However, the reception we got at Love Street was unexpected and frightening. We were expecting a fight with St Mirren and we were swaggering around as though we were invincible, but what happened next was unbelievable. We were in the shed next to the fence separating both sets of supporters, taunting St Mirren and bouncing about like a bunch of excited kids when all of a sudden there was a chant of 'Casuals, Casuals, get tae fuck!' This wasn't from St Mirren but from our own fans who were beginning to surround us in a very menacing way. The average age of our mob was about 16, and here we were, surrounded by drink-fuelled veterans of the terrace who apparently hated us.

A couple of skirmishes broke out and we were chased on to the track by the scarfers. The police intervened and escorted us out of the stadium and to the train station, where we were herded on to the first train to Glasgow. A couple of lads were nursing black eyes and bloody noses.

The rest of the day was pretty uneventful and ended with a few of us going for a pint in order to discuss plans for the next game and what we had learned from the day's events. We got knock-backs from all the pubs in the city centre so we eventually decided to try an Irish bar on the south side of the Jamaica Bridge. It was called the Country Corner and we got in without any trouble. We talked about our unexpected enemy – the Celtic support – a support that guarded its reputation and good name with a passion that we hadn't reckoned with, even as Celtic supporters ourselves.

The St Mirren game was in January 1985, just weeks after the shocking events that surrounded a European Cup Winners' Cup match against Rapid Vienna. These were the darkest days in Celtic's proud European history. Having disposed of Belgium's Ghent in the first round, Celtic were paired with Austria's Rapid Vienna in the next round. The first leg was played in Vienna in October 1984, with Rapid recording a 3–1 win. Celtic were optimistic about progressing, thanks to the away goal scored by Brian McLair. The second leg was at Celtic Park on 7 November 1984. An expectant crowd turned up in numbers and weren't disappointed as Celtic went 2–0 ahead, with goals from Brian McLair and Murdo Macleod, in a fantastic first half.

After the break, Tommy Burns made it 3–0 with about 20 minutes to go. The game looked a foregone conclusion when Celtic were awarded a penalty five minutes after the Burns goal. The Rapid players surrounded the referee, who was consulting his linesman on the Jungle side of the pitch. Suddenly, one of the Rapid players fell to the ground as if he had been struck by a sniper's bullet. He lay there for over 10 minutes before leaving the field covered in bandages. Peter Grant then missed the penalty, screwing his shot wide – understandable, given he had waited 15 minutes to take the kick. Celtic held on to their 3–0 lead and were looking forward to the next round.

The following day, news broke that Rapid had complained to UEFA, claiming their player had been struck with a bottle thrown from the crowd in the Jungle. TV pictures, which UEFA apparently never viewed, clearly showed a bottle landing on the pitch but nowhere near any Rapid players. Incredibly, UEFA ordered the match to be replayed with the venue instructed to be over 100km outside Glasgow. Old Trafford was the chosen venue.

The largest travelling support for an away European tie, 40,000-plus, made the journey south. Celtic inevitably lost the match 1–0, with Rapid scoring from a breakaway following a Celtic corner, from which Roy Aitkin rattled the post so hard that the ball rebounded upfield to an unmarked Rapid player, who sprinted away unchallenged to score the only goal of the game. As the match passed away, tensions got to some of the Celtic fans with at least three separate people running on to the pitch in an attempt to attack the Rapid players. Celtic were punished again by UEFA and ordered to play their next European home game behind closed doors. As for Rapid, they made it all the way to the final, where they were beaten by Everton.

The emergence of a group of Casuals was the last thing the Celtic fans wanted. They knew that any adverse publicity connected to crowd trouble could result in Celtic being banned altogether by UEFA. As the Crew developed, so did the disapproval aimed at us from the Celtic support. They made it clear that the Casuals were not welcome.

I discovered how deep their feelings ran when, a few weeks after the St Mirren match, I was arrested during a Celtic v Morton match at Cappielow. The Celtic Soccer Crew had taken up position in the seated area behind one of the goals. The majority of scarfers were in the ramshackle shed that runs the length of the pitch. Every time there was a lull in the action on the pitch, the scarfers turned their attention to us, with the all-too-familiar chant of 'Casuals, Casuals, get to fuck'. I decided to stand up amongst our Crew and reply by trying to start a chorus of a Celtic song. I had hardly completed the first few lines – 'We are Celtic supporters, faithful through and through' – when I was grabbed by two uniformed officers and arrested. This brought the biggest cheer of the day from the Celtic support. I was led through a gate and on to the trackside. The police gate was less than 20 yards away to the right-hand side of where we were sitting. However, the police decided to take me the long way round past the shed with the scarfers in it. As I was nearing the shed, an assortment of missiles was being thrown from the scarfers in my direction. There were half-eaten pies, coins, lighters and, worst of all, spit all coming from the shed. Fortunately for me, I was flanked by the two policemen who were taking the brunt of the barrage. They hurried me along, and we eventually reached the police gate where I was put into a waiting van and taken to the police station.

I was let out later that night and appeared in court a few months later, where I was fined £20 for allegedly shouting, 'Fuck off, we're the Casuals, come ahead.' It amazes me that, when the police exaggerate in court (I won't say *lie*, because, as everybody knows, the police don't tell lies), they always come up with some ridiculous chant that no one would ever shout.

The Celtic fans kept up their display of disapproval against the Crew for a couple of seasons. However, they always seemed very quiet if they were on the football specials that used to be the Celtic Soccer Crew's preferred mode of transport.

The things we did achieve in those early days, however, would go on to play a major part in my life for the next 20 years. We had created a mob that lacked leadership and guidance. This was due to the fact that we had people from different housing schemes who didn't trust one another because of the history of territorial gang fighting in Glasgow. It also has to be admitted that we attracted some nutters and undesirables who were only interested in robbing many of the younger well-dressed recruits of their money and belongings.

Throughout the next couple of weeks, we grew from the initial 70 to a mob of hundreds. A group of us recognised that we needed organisation and started to produce a newsletter that we distributed among the various crews. Looking back on it now, it seems very naive and looks like jail bait, especially in the light of the undercover operations that the police had mounted in England in a bid to stamp out football hooliganism. We did, however, manage to establish a certain level of control over the Crew.

The next step was to set up a base where we could meet regularly. We decided upon the Country Corner as it was close to the city centre, and meant that people from the various schemes could meet without fear of attack from rival gangs. The pub was basically a bit of a dive, but most of us were allowed to drink there, even though many of us were underage. The Country Corner would play a major part in the growth of the Celtic Casuals.

We then had to decide on a name, and I hold up my

hands and wholeheartedly apologise for coming up with the original title of Roman Catholic Casuals. This lasted for the first couple of months until it became apparent that half the mob was Protestant!

We decided to change the name and a lot of suggestions were put forward for consideration. This ranged from the Celtic Soccer Trendies – which if you'd seen half our mob you'd realise how inappropriate that title was – to us toying with the name COSH – Celtic's Organised Soccer Hooligans – which was also dismissed. We eventually decided to go with CSC – Celtic Soccer Crew – and the name has stuck with us ever since.

The Country Corner was now recognised as our base to such an extent that we would continue to meet there for a drink when there wasn't a game on. The owner was a big Irish guy who was willing to bend the rules for a quick profit. He did, however, draw the line with those among us who looked just that bit too young to be in a pub. This led to a large crowd of younger lads feeling a bit left out of things. They began to meet around the city centre and soon established the Celtic Baby Crew. Another group of lads would not be seen in the Country Corner, and they found a pub in the city centre, which led to us nicknaming them the Sylvester's Shirties. This in effect meant that we had three separate mobs, meeting at different locations, and there was a complete lack of communication and leadership. This led to us being turned over by most that came to Celtic Park.

Our trips to away matches, however, were much more fruitful. This was mainly due to the football specials that were put on for football supporters to travel to and from games at a special cheap rate. One day in particular, we were due to play Kilmarnock at Rugby Park and had arranged to meet inside Central Station. It was a week of snow and frost and inevitably the match was called off the day before. We were at a loss and wondering where to go, when someone suggested that we should head to Carlisle, who happened to be playing Millwall that Saturday.

These were the days before mobile phones and it was quite an achievement that we managed to gather 30 lads together at such short notice. We met early the next morning and travelled first-class on the InterCity train, much to the annoyance of the middle-class businessmen who normally had the first-class compartments to themselves and who expected to have a quiet journey.

There were about 30 of us on the train, but others had decided to make their own way to Carlisle by car and bus and meet up with the rest of us there. We hadn't left Glasgow unnoticed, though, and were greeted in Carlisle by the local constabulary. We got off the train and were lined up against a wall where we were all searched and had our carry-outs confiscated. Me and my mate Joey were arrested because we only had children's tickets. We were given the option of either paying for full adult tickets or being charged with fraud. We didn't have enough money between us to pay for the tickets, so it looked like we were going to miss out on the day's fun, but then to our surprise one of the officers who had been searching the others came into the office and said that our mates had had a whip-round and paid for our tickets.

We were soon on the streets of Carlisle causing mayhem. We found a pub on the main street and quickly had it under control. A few Carlisle lads were soon on the scene to check us out. They were more inquisitive than threatening. Carlisle told us that Millwall were due in at about 2pm and asked us to team up with them and have a go at the Londoners. There was an uneasy truce established but we could already sense that it wasn't going to last.

The numbers on both sides grew steadily as more lads arrived. The pub was absolutely mobbed and it wasn't long before the police arrived to take up positions outside. This was a new experience for the Celtic boys. In Glasgow, the police would have entered the pub and arrested anyone that even looked at them the wrong way. The Carlisle cops seemed more content to contain us in a large crowd without risking confrontation.

Our mob now numbered about 40, because a few of the Shirties had made their own way down after hearing about our trip. At 2pm, both mobs left the pub and attempted to get to the train station, but the police had every move covered. A group of about 50–100

Millwall had travelled by train and were escorted on to buses waiting for them at the station. We had no chance of a pop at Millwall, which was probably just as well, as they looked old enough to be our dads!

Our disappointment was to be short-lived, as we decided to have a go at Carlisle instead. The tension had been building all day and it didn't take much prompting for us to kick it off. I think we took them by surprise as they were quickly on their toes. The police were also taken by surprise as they had been concentrating on keeping us away from Millwall. A couple of Carlisle did try to stand but they were easily dealt with – and Celtic's first victory on English soil was won. None of our lads was injured or lifted in the fight.

The police were uncertain about what to do with us. If they'd had any brains, they would have put us on the first available train back to Glasgow. But what they did next was unbelievable. For some unknown reason, they decided to open a terrace behind one of the goals – just for us! What followed is one of the most bizarre things I have ever experienced in a football stadium. Carlisle were in the shed to our left, with the tartan-rug brigade in the main stand to our right. I can't remember where the small pocket of Millwall were put in the stadium.

We decided that, as we were there, we might as well enjoy ourselves, so we started a lung-bursting rendition of 'You'll Never Walk Alone'. A couple of lads had brought banners with them and some had scarves. I don't know what the locals made of us, but I could safely say that anyone who was at the match would most likely have forgotten the score by now, but will still be able to recall the antics of the Celtic lads that day. The craziest thing we did was when we all stripped to the waist and performed a conga up and down the terrace. This was met with rapturous applause from all the other fans in the ground.

At the end of the match, the police held us in the ground until the rest of the crowd had left. When they eventually let us out, the escort outnumbered us! We were entirely surrounded by police and had no chance of sneaking away. When we got to the city centre, we noticed large groups of Carlisle milling around, but they made no attempt to attack us. We were escorted all the way to the train station and on to the platform. The majority of the police escort, however, remained at the entrance to prevent us from slipping back out and into town.

We were just standing around feeling quite pleased with the day's events when suddenly a crowd of Carlisle came charging towards us from the car-park exit ramp. After the ease of our previous victory, we were well up for it and steamed right into them. Carlisle made a better attempt this time, but were nothing much. We soon had them on their toes again and heading back out of the station.

When we returned to the platform, we were met with

applause and chants of 'Bushwhacker, Bushwhacker' coming from the adjacent platform where Millwall were waiting for their train back to London. After a few minutes, our train arrived and we were on our way back to Glasgow with plenty of back-slapping and bragging to keep us going all the way home. We were all on an incredible high after what we had achieved that day.

CHAPTER 3

Season 1985–86 will be remembered as one of the most dramatic in the history of Scottish football, marking the end of one era and the dawn of a new one. The season was only about five weeks old when Scottish football was rocked by the news of the great Jock Stein's sudden death. Mr Stein was in Cardiff with the Scotland team for a crucial World Cup qualifier against Wales. If I remember correctly, Scotland secured a 1–1 draw which was enough to see us qualify for the 1986 finals in Mexico. As the game was drawing to a close, Big Jock complained of chest pains before collapsing, having suffered a fatal heart attack.

The news of his death rocked the football world, with tributes coming from every corner of the globe in acknowledgement of his tremendous contribution to the game. Big Jock was responsible for revolutionising football in Scotland. His philosophy of free-flowing attacking football paid dividends with Celtic being crowned European Champions in 1967. He also guided Celtic to nine consecutive League titles, a world record at the time.

Three days after his death, Celtic played host to defending champions Aberdeen in a crucial top-of-the-table clash, which resulted in a 2–1 victory for Celtic. The match, however, will be remembered more poignantly for the fantastic gesture shown by the Aberdeen fans that day. There had been an impeccably observed minute's silence before the kick-off. When the referee blew his whistle to signal the end of the tribute, a group of Aberdeen fans walked on to the running track and headed towards the pitch. At first the Celtic fans thought that it was an attempt by Aberdeen Casuals to invade the pitch. However, although there appeared to be members of the ASC amongst the half-dozen or so in the group, the last thing on their mind was to tarnish the big man's name. The Aberdeen contingent paid their respect to Mr Stein by laying a wreath behind one of the goals. This demonstrated the respect and affection that all true football fans had for the greatest-ever Celtic manager.

As the 1985–86 season progressed, it looked likely that Hearts would emerge as Champions. The Edinburgh side had gone on an incredible unbeaten run which began before the turn of the year. Celtic were the only team that could realistically pip Hearts to the title, but we looked to have blown our chances when the team recorded four draws in a row, the last one being against Rangers at Ibrox on 22 March 1986 where the two sides shared the points in an eight-goal thriller. I would say that the 4–4 game was one of the best Old Firm games that I have ever had the pleasure of witnessing, purely from a football point of view. But it is one of the worst experiences that I have ever had to endure when it comes to the football violence side of things.

We had a massive Crew that day, as did Rangers and their ICF. On our journey to Ibrox, our firm numbered about 400. We were in a police escort and the chances of having a go at the ICF were limited, although there were sporadic outbursts of violence. When we arrived at the stadium, our Crew had to break up into loads of different groups. This was due to the large number of tickets that Celtic used to be allocated in the days before the Souness revolution which saw thousands of glory-hunters flock to Ibrox. This meant that, in addition to the traditional Broomloan Stand, we were also given tickets for sections of the Govan Stand, main stand and enclosure, in total about 17,000 briefs.

Back in the 80s, genuine Celtic fans could afford to attend most games and easily purchased tickets from the club's public sale which operated a first come, first served basis, unlike today when a lot of ordinary fans can't get tickets for Old Firm matches due to the amount of briefs that go to investor-level season ticket holders and corporate guests.

After the match, it was already kicking off before most of our Crew had even got out of the stadium. The Celtic lads who didn't have tickets had been in a pub, the Mucky Duck, which was on Broomloan Road close to the junction with Paisley Road. When the final whistle went, they had left the pub and were involved in running battles with Rangers fans and some ICF. Some of the lads who were at the game managed to reach the place where the battle was going on just as the police arrived. The coppers surrounded the Celtic Crew, which numbered several hundred, and hemmed them in with help from the mounted division, preventing any of the lads from slipping away. That left about 80 of our Crew who hadn't been involved in the fracas. We didn't fancy attracting the same attention from the police that the majority of the Crew were getting.

In an effort to escape any police escort, we decided to make our way across the bridge that took us into Dumbreck, an affluent area on the south side of Glasgow, separated from the poorer Ibrox area by the M8 motorway. The plan was to head through the quiet streets towards a footbridge that would bring us back across the M8 and on to Paisley Road, close to the Cessnock Underground Station. There were about 20 younger boys with us who were members of the Celtic Baby Crew. I think they felt they needed to prove themselves to the older boys in the Crew. When we turned on to the road that would lead us to the footbridge, we noticed groups of Rangers fans making their way home from the match. The Babes decided to have a go at the Rangers fans and began to chase them towards the bridge. The rest of us in the Crew knew that it was not worth our while chasing scarfers.

Meanwhile, the Babes had reached the footbridge and followed the running Rangers fans on to it. They were by now a good distance in front of us when we heard the distinctive wail of police sirens, becoming louder the closer we got to the bridge. At this point, we could see the Babes involved in a battle with older Rangers scarfers, who seemed to have come to the rescue of the ones that had been chased by the Baby Crew. As the 60 or so of us got to the access point of the bridge, a police car, quickly followed by a van, mounted the pavement in front of us blocking our way on to the footbridge with the vehicles.

What happened next is one of the most sickening experiences that I have ever witnessed. A number of the ICF had now joined in the battle against the Celtic Baby Crew, who were attempting to put up a good fight. The ICF then fired a flare into the 20 or so Babes, which forced them to take to their toes and run back towards the end of the bridge where we were. However, one of the Baby Crew had tripped and fallen to the ground. He was soon surrounded by the Rangers mob and was taking a really bad beating. Those of us who were being prevented from going on the bridge surged forward in an attempt to break through the police line. The coppers drew their truncheons, making it impossible for anyone to go to our mate's help. We could do nothing but stand there helpless as we watched a couple of the Rangers lads pick up the Celtic Babe and toss him over the footbridge railing. Thank God, he was close to the far end of the bridge, meaning he landed on the sloping grass embankment and not on one of the eight lanes of the M8 motorway.

I felt particularly responsible because the young lad who received that terrible beating would probably not have been involved with the Celtic hooligans if he had not been in the same children's home as me. We didn't get an opportunity that day for our revenge on the ICF for what they had done. We would, however, have an unexpected chance about six weeks later.

The 4–4 draw at Ibrox was the last game that Celtic would drop points that season. The team won seven games in a row before going into the final game against St Mirren at Love Street. We still needed a minor miracle to stop Hearts from winning the title. They were two points ahead and had a better goal difference of four goals going into their final game away to Dundee. The Celtic support travelled to Love Street more in hope than expectation. The team certainly believed that, if they did their job, then anything could happen at Dens Park. Celtic were simply unstoppable that day and were 4–0 up at half-time. Meanwhile, in Dundee, the score remained at 0–0 after 45 minutes –

there was still hope. Celtic scored a fifth before the hour mark, but knew it still wouldn't be enough unless Hearts lost. These were the days before three points for a win were introduced, so a draw would be enough for Hearts to clinch the title by one point.

With the games heading into the final 10 minutes, all attention was focused on events in Dundee. Hundreds of fans had radios pressed to their ears, while others crowded round for any information. Then suddenly the place erupted: Dundee had scored with seven minutes to go and the scorer was Kidd. There was then a hushed silence as confusion revolved around the identity of the goalscorer: was it Albert Kidd of Dundee or Walter Kidd of Hearts? It didn't matter because the next goal scored made it 2–0 to Dundee and again it had been Kidd, but there was no doubt the Kidd in question was Albert of Dundee.

I will never forget that day; the vision that will live with me forever is the moment that the St Mirren goalkeeper was about to release the ball from his hands and punt it upfield. However, he aborted his kick and held on to the ball as the Celtic fans erupted when news of the second Dundee goal filtered through. That day is the best that I have ever experienced as a Celtic supporter. The scenes at the end of the match will live with me forever. It was the most incredible feeling, bettered only by the birth of my children.

The 1985–86 season had begun with the passing of the man who had revolutionised the game, marking the end of an era when Jock Stein sadly passed away. By way of remarkable coincidence, the end of the 1985–86 season marked the dawn of a new revolution and the beginning of a very different era which would see the Scottish game changed forever. Our biggest rivals from across the city announced that ex-Scotland International and Liverpool legend Graeme Souness had agreed to join Rangers as player/manager. His appointment was big news and added a greater importance to the Glasgow Cup Final which was due to be played at Ibrox on 9 May 1986, just six days after that remarkable day in Paisley.

The Glasgow Cup is a competition normally played amongst the reserves or under-21 teams of the five Glasgow clubs, the Old Firm along with Clyde, Queens Park and Partick Thistle. When Souness took charge, his first announcement stated that he wanted to have a look at the first-team players and would field a strong side against Celtic.

The match was played on a Friday night, which in itself is unusual for an Old Firm game. For our Crew, it was ideal and made the job of meeting up in large numbers a lot easier, as we were able to mingle in with the usual Friday-night crowds who filled the Glasgow pubs from 5pm onwards.

The memory of what happened back in March was still fresh in our minds and we vowed that we wouldn't make the same mistakes this time. The plan was for several meeting places in various pubs in the city centre that could accommodate up to 50 lads at a time without drawing too much attention.

At about 6.30pm, the various groups were to make their way to the agreed meeting point, which was at the bandstand on the River Clyde Walkway. Once we had grouped up, we had a firm in excess of 300. We made our way from the city centre and towards Ibrox, walking down one-way streets into the oncoming traffic, which we hoped would allow us to avoid a police escort. We knew we had a good Crew and we were determined to put on a good show.

We got to the Kingston Bridge, which is about two miles from Ibrox, without attracting an escort. There were some policemen on foot but still no sign of the vanloads or the mounted division which usually accompanied us on our journey to Ibrox Stadium. As we passed under the Kingston Bridge, there were some missiles being tossed at us from Rangers scarfers who had come out of a pub close to Paisley Road toll. The scarfers, however, were content just to throw the various objects at us before retreating into the relative safety of the pub, pulling down the shutters in the process. The general feeling amongst our Crew was to ignore the scarfers in the pub. We knew that we had done well to get this far without attracting an escort.

As we got closer to Paisley Road toll, you could sense the tension building amongst the Crew; the old boys were barking out instructions, telling everyone to close in and for the younger ones to take up position in the middle of the Crew. For the majority of lads in the CSC that night, it was the first time that we had attempted to walk down Paisley Road without the relative safety that a police escort provides. We could see people pouring out of the pubs that lined both sides of the road ahead and stood between us and Ibrox Stadium. The Crew began to sing some song in an effort to stir up the troops and get the adrenalin pumping as we prepared ourselves for the gauntlet that we were about to run. The Rangers fans outnumbered us by at least 5:1, but they weren't acting as one unit, whereas we were. We stuck together and managed to fight off the Rangers scarfers who were attempting to attack us.

The atmosphere was very intimidating and volatile, but nevertheless we managed to get past all the pubs without any casualties. Although we hadn't turned over the Rangers scarfers or taken one of their pubs, the Crew still felt that we had achieved a moral victory gained by the simple fact we stuck together and maintained a certain level of discipline. We had now reached the fork in Paisley Road; one way continues as Paisley Road and would have been the sensible route for us to take as it meets with Broomloan Road, which is the traditional Celtic end, whereas the other way takes you to Edmiston Drive past the main entrance to Ibrox Stadium and is the preferred route for Rangers fans. Buoyed up by our success at passing all the pubs relatively unscathed, we decided to head down

Edmiston Drive and not just with the usual singing and goading; some wisecrack in our Crew thought that it would be a laugh if we all put our arms around each other's shoulders and sang the Sinatra classic 'New York, New York'. I think the Rangers scarfers were so bemused by our antics that they thought better of challenging us.

We eventually got to the Celtic end and made plans for everybody to leave the match just before the end. However, after 90 minutes, the score was 2–2 meaning there would be 30 minutes' extra-time and possibly penalties. Ally McCoist scored his and Rangers third to secure a 3–2 win for the home team. The majority of our Crew still had the sense to make their way to the exits before the final whistle sounded. We grouped up and headed towards the junction of Paisley Road and Broomloan Road. The ICF, who had been anonymous before the match, suddenly appeared from one of the side streets; they must have had about 200–300 in their firm, about the same number as us. A good toe-to-toe battle developed with flares and other missiles being discharged by both Crews. Although it was an Old Firm match with a capacity crowd, the police appeared to be unprepared. It was as if they had treated the match as a reserve fixture and had deployed only a limited number of officers in accordance with what would normally be required.

The battle raged on for what seemed an age. A couple of policemen on motorbikes tried to intervene, but soon realised that their efforts were more likely to put themselves in danger, especially when one of the motorbikes with the cop still on board was knocked to the ground as he tried to separate the two mobs by driving into the middle of the melee. Reinforcements eventually arrived and began arresting large numbers from both sides. Luckily for me and a few others, we managed to escape to the safety of one of our Crew's house which was in one of the flats that made up the housing scheme directly outside Ibrox Stadium. Strangely enough, there were a number of Celtic lads who lived in the vicinity of Ibrox Stadium, while a large proportion of the ICF hail from the East End of Glasgow.

It was by now the end of season 1986–87. Our final League game was against Hearts at Tynecastle. A crowd of us had decided to travel through early and do a pub crawl along Corstorphine. There must have been about 30 of us, but it was all game boys with a couple of girls in tow. We arrived in Edinburgh at about eleven in the morning and got off the bus near the zoo. We were on a mission and out to cause as much trouble as possible.

We went into a couple of pubs but were asked to leave after our first pint. A few lads threw their glasses about, but there wasn't that much disorder. A couple of our lads decided to rob an off-sales for a drink, while the rest of us went to a pub called The Roseburn, which is a traditional Hearts pub. The Hearts mob must have heard about our early arrival and were soon on the scene but not in big numbers. A few lads left the pub to confront them but they ran off. We decided to stay at this pub and wait for the rest of our Crew coming off the train.

A short time later, Hearts came back towards the pub with what they must have regarded as a mob capable of turning us over. What they didn't know was a few of us were carrying flares. We left the pub and were soon involved in a fierce battle. It was absolute chaos with flares going off and various weapons being used. We would have been turned over if it wasn't for the hand-held flares that we had. The fight went on quite long in football terms until the police showed up.

I wasn't aware of it happening, but it soon became clear that a Hearts lad had been badly cut up and stabbed. The police had us lined up against a wall and conducted an impromptu ID parade. Frank and his girlfriend were first to be picked out, the main reason being his girl was from Edinburgh and had run with Hearts. I was next to be pointed out along with one other guy, McLean. At this point, we didn't know what was happening because, although Frank and I had used the flares, none of us had been involved in the slashing.

We were taken to the West End Police Station and held until the Tuesday when we would appear in court. The Hearts bird, Nic, got out as she was pregnant. This was a godsend to us, as she was able to provide us with food and refreshments and organise legal representation. The three of us weren't unduly worried as we knew it was a set-up and they would soon realise their mistake.

We were held in a massive cell along with three Hibs boys who got arrested later on. When they first came into the cell, the atmosphere was uneasy. However, after a while, we were talking and even playing football against each other. We made a ball from sponge we took from a mattress and wrapped up in a carrier bag. We were that confident of getting out that we made the most of the time we had to spend in the cells.

With Nic on the outside, she was able to organise legal representation and Frank received a visit from a top lawyer in Edinburgh. It wasn't good news, as we were informed we were facing charges of serious assault and firearms, due to the flares. We were given some hope, though, as we learned that a couple of girls who had been with us had taken photos of the fighting and they could be in our favour.

On the Tuesday morning, we were taken to Edinburgh Sheriff Court where the three of us were put in a holding cell together. We were then served with an indictment, which was all new to us and we didn't quite understand what was happening.

The three of us had been charged with assault to inflict severe injury and danger to life, and also under possession of firearms and breach of the peace. We were all very nervous and the fun and games which we had enjoyed in the cell at the weekend now seemed like a distant memory. The lawyer came to see us one at a time and tried to outline the procedure. We all protested our innocence but were told we would only be allowed to confirm our names and addresses at court and no plea would be tendered. I asked about bail, but he told me we would concentrate on that at the next hearing. I really didn't understand but put my trust in him as he seemed to know what he was talking about.

Just after 2pm, we were taken into court where Nic joined us in the dock. The procedure was very brief, with the result we were remanded in custody for further enquiries to be carried out. We were led back to a cell to await transport to Saughton Prison. None of us had ever been in prison before and to be honest we were very apprehensive about the prospect of going to jail. News of our fight and consequent arrest must have filtered through to the cons in Saughton and we were to receive a very hostile reception.

A prison officer warned us to be on our guard and offered to put us on protection. We declined the offer and vowed to stick together. We were shown into one of the halls of the Victorian prison. It was very intimidating as we were the only Glaswegians. As we walked to our cell on the bottom flat, curious cons were leaning over the various railings on the landings to get a good view of the new arrivals. We were only in the cell a couple of minutes when a con came in and told Frank to take his trainers off. I slammed the cell door shut and told him to try to take them. He quickly said he was only kidding and pressed the buzzer to be let out.

Later that evening, Frank and I were told we had visitors. We went to the visiting room and were put in a separate section used for closed visits. As I made my way to my allotted table, I was surprised to be greeted by two Hibs boys. One was named after a cartoon train and the other I will call the Fat Controller due to the fact he's fat and likes to think he can control things. I soon told them to fuck off. Frank's parents and his girlfriend were there to see him, and his mum and dad came over to my table on seeing that I was sitting alone.

Frank's dad told me they had got hold of the photos and were going to give them to the lawyer. This lifted our spirits as he said some photos showed Frank and me with flares in our hands on the opposite side of the road to where the guy had been slashed. Although they didn't show who was attacking the guy, they showed that it couldn't have been Frank or me, or indeed McLeany.

The following day, the three of us were transferred to Polmont Young Offenders' Institution. This was totally different to Saughton as there were loads of Glaswegians in the wings. However, we were taken to south wing, which is exclusively for remand prisoners who had been through courts on the east coast and south of Scotland.

We spent just over a week in Polmont without incident and awaited our return to court with enthusiasm, as we believed we would be released. When we got to court, the lawyer told us he would be applying for bail, but to be warned that the Crown was opposing our release. We asked about the photos but he told us he was keeping them for the trial as at that point they could work against us.

I couldn't understand this but he assured me that out of the three of us I was most likely to get bail, so I went along with him. Again, we were to appear in a closed court, and one by one our bail was refused, apart from Nic who was pregnant.

The words of the judge that day went through my head for the next four months. He spoke to me and started with the words, 'Mr O'Kane, you have a very strong case for bail.' I listened with anticipation, awaiting the words saying I could go. But my heart sank when he continued with the word 'but'. I knew right away my application was refused. We were taken back to the cell where we found it hard to look each other in the eye, as the three of us were shattered.

The lawyer came and told us he would try for High Court bail and again not to worry. We were taken back to Polmont and faced up to the fact we could be spending the next 16 weeks behind bars. We clung to the slim hope of High Court bail and our hopes were raised when after about five days the three of us were taken out of our cells to the PO's office to receive news regarding our appeal. What happened next left us numb.

Frank was told to collect his belongings while McLeany and I were told our appeal was turned down. It was totally surreal with Frank elated and us two absolutely gutted. We helped Frank pack and divided his provisions between us. The first couple of weeks after that day were hard. However, the support we received from family and friends was reassuring. Frank and a couple of lads came up to see me soon after his release. He told me the lawyer had done a deal to secure his release, sacrificing me and McLeany. I immediately dropped this lawyer and asked for my own brief team from Pollok.

We soon settled into our remand and looked forward to our day in court. While on remand, my lawyer advised me to write to the courts and ask for my outstanding fines to be taken into consideration and impose the relevant sentence, meaning I would be transferred to the convicted wing for a while. I had almost forgotten about this and was in my cell one day expecting a visit from my parents when I was told to pack my stuff, as I was moving to do the time for the fines.

I told the officer my mum and dad were coming to see me and asked if they would get in I was now seen as a convicted prisoner. He said they wouldn't be allowed as I would have to have sent a pass and those visits were weekends only. I explained my mother was ill and it would be her only visit. I was taken to see the governor and, after much pleading, he allowed my parents in.

This was probably the most emotional visit I ever had, as my mum said she believed that I hadn't stabbed anyone and would back me up 100 per cent. This really lifted my spirits and when I got the revised charge sheet with the date to appear at the High Court I was very confident. The charge against me was now the assault and nothing else.

This puzzled me, as I'd made no secret of the fact I was on the other side of the road wielding a flare. The date was fast approaching and we were told they were taking us to Saughton the Friday before the proposed date. I hadn't been in any trouble in the four months I spent in Polmont until the day before I was due to go to Saughton.

I was in the exercise yard when a Hearts lad who had just come in was trying to wind me up about what would happen to me in Saughton. The main reason I hadn't been in much trouble was I wasn't prepared to take any shit and let the others know that. But this guy went too far, resulting in me decking him.

The next day, we were off down to Saughton, looking forward to the trial, and we weren't too apprehensive about what reception we would get this time as we had wised up with the time spent in Polmont. McLeany and me went to the dining hall for lunch where I was approached by a couple of guys who told me I would be stabbed if I came out of my cell that night. One of them then lifted his shirt to reveal a crude dagger-like weapon stuck down the front of his trousers. He said the guy I had decked in Polmont was his cousin and I was getting it.

We went back to the cell and discussed what I should do. I was shitting myself but decided to go out to face the music after weighing up the options. I realised, if I didn't go out and things didn't go my way at trial, then my life would be unbearable if I received a sentence.

We went to the dining hall and were soon approached by the goons. My plan was to use my metal tray as a cosh if they tried anything. The guy came up to me and offered me his hand, saying he respected the fact I hadn't backed down and if I experienced any more trouble then I should let him know. I was really relieved and pleased that I now had one less problem to worry about.

We were taken to court on the Monday but they weren't ready to start, so we returned to Saughton until the Thursday morning. Unbeknown to me, my lawyer was doing a lot of negotiating behind the scenes and had acquired a set of the photos. When we got to court on the Thursday, they told us the trial would start that day. We were being held in a large room instead of the cells. This added to the importance of the occasion. Just before lunch, my lawyer came in and told me that the Crown was willing to accept my plea of not guilty after seeing the photos.

I didn't know whether to laugh or cry as we had this evidence from the start. The escorting officers led us to the steps to the courtroom, which was resplendent in all its pomp and grandeur. We were told to stand in order of age, with Nic being oldest and Frank youngest. I was number three. The charges were read out. We had to tender our pleas in order. Nic replied guilty to one charge and not to the others. McLeany pleaded not guilty to all, as did I. Frank pleaded to two charges but not guilty to the assault. The prosecutor replied to the pleas by saying that the pleas of number one and number three were acceptable. I stood there in a trance-like state not believing what I was hearing. The judge, who was sitting high above us decked out in red robes and a wig, looking very authoritative, addressed me with the immortal words, 'Mr O'Kane, you are free to leave.'

I was taken back down to the holding room where I was told I would be released once they had carried out a warrant check. I waited for about an hour when an officer told me, 'Sorry, I've bad news, you've a warrant outstanding for failing to appear at court in Glasgow.'

I was stunned but wasn't too bothered, as it was the district court and after what I had been through I was just happy to be heading back west.

I was taken to a holding cell to await transport to take me to Glasgow. As I was waiting, I received a very emotional visit from my parents. It took a great deal of effort for my mum to make the journey to Edinburgh, given that she rarely left her bed, let alone the house. Also, considering all the turmoil that had dominated my relationship with my mum and the disagreements that existed between my mum and dad, it was a fantastic gesture by both of them to put all their differences aside and support me on a united front. I was allowed to spend about five minutes with my parents. There were a lot of tears in between hugs and it is a moment that will live with me forever.

When my mum and dad had gone, I was in the cell for about an hour before the police from Glasgow arrived to escort me to Stewart Street Police Station, which is in Glasgow city centre. I appeared in court on the Friday morning feeling rather overdressed. I was still wearing the suit and shirt that my dad had bought me for the High Court. I was fined a couple of hundred pounds and was now free. It was a fantastic feeling walking out of the court and into the August sunshine.

The next day Celtic were playing Rangers at Celtic Park. It was also my dad's 50th birthday and there was a party planned for that night. Frank, who was in the dock with me in Edinburgh, had received a deferred sentence after having his charges dropped to a breach. He had got tickets for the match and asked me if I wanted to go with him. My girlfriend at the time, Rita, and my dad weren't happy about me going to the game. I promised them that I wouldn't get into any trouble and that Frank's dad was going with us. I met up with Frank at his house where we had a few beers before heading to Celtic Park. We decided to get a taxi to avoid any possibility of running into any trouble. The match itself had all the excitement and passion of an Old Firm derby, with Celtic winning 1–0 thanks to an early goal from Billy Stark.

After the match, we headed into the city centre. Frank's dad wasn't with us as he had a ticket for the stand while ours were for the terrace, meaning that, even though we planned to see him after the game, we couldn't get to the agreed meeting point because of the enormous amount of people exiting the ground at the same time. There was only four or five of us and we were heading towards Frank's house. As we were cutting through George Square, a fight broke out near by. I decided I didn't want to get involved and began to run in the opposite direction from where the fight was. As I turned a corner, I ran straight into two coppers who were responding to the fight. They grabbed me and asked why I was running. I tried to explain that I was trying to get away from the trouble. They took a look at me and concluded I was involved in the fight based solely on the fact I wasn't wearing a scarf but had on a Lacoste jumper with a Celtic button badge on it, which to them identified me as a Casual.

I was arrested and taken to Stewart Street Police Station, where I had left the previous morning on my way to the court. On arrival at the charge desk, the sergeant told me that I would get out that night once my address was verified. I told them it was my dad's 50th birthday party and I was expected to be there. I pleaded with them not to contact my dad as it would ruin his night, adding that I had only left Stewart Street the previous day. The desk sergeant remembered me as he was on duty when I was brought in on the Thursday. He said that there would be no need to confirm my address and he therefore wouldn't contact my dad. He promised that I would be let out once they had processed the other people who had been arrested after the match.

I was in a cell for about an hour when, true to his word, the desk sergeant allowed me out. I got home in time to get changed before going to the party, where I had a great time without anyone knowing that I had been arrested.

CHAPTER 4

Season 1987–88 was a momentous one for Celtic with the club celebrating its centenary. It was also a season that saw the CSC claim some notable victories, the first of which was on English soil – against Scottish opposition this time.

The last weekend in September is a traditional holiday for the people of Glasgow and usually results in a mass exodus to Blackpool. A large crowd of Celtic lads had decided we would go down for the weekend and let our hair down. Most of the Crew left on the Friday morning to get the benefit of the full weekend, but a few of us couldn't make it until the Saturday due to work commitments.

We arrived in Blackpool at about lunchtime on the Saturday and made our way to the digs where most of the boys were staying. We quickly found out about events the previous night and the running battles that had taken place with Motherwell, who had a healthy mob down with them. According to reports, our crowd had come across Motherwell outside a club at the Central Pier. At first there wasn't any fighting but just the usual banter, until somebody from our mob tossed a glass into the Motherwell boys. Motherwell steamed in and chased Celtic to a pub where most of our lads were drinking. They came out on hearing the commotion and soon a good toe-to-toe fight was in progress, until the police arrived and began arresting some lads. The two sides were separated, with the Celtic lads being escorted along the promenade to their digs.

With us arriving on the Saturday, our numbers totalled about 30, along with the addition of a couple of Hibs boys who had come down. I wasn't happy about their presence as one of them was the Fat Controller who had come up to Saughton to see me. I left it for the moment, as our main concern was dealing with Motherwell.

It was decided we would attack their hotel, as we knew where they were staying. We split into three groups of about 10, with one crowd going direct to the front entrance to entice them out, and the other two crowds lying in wait at opposite sides of the hotel. On seeing our crowd at their door, Motherwell came steaming out and fell perfectly into our trap. We soon had them running for cover back indoors and some lads followed them. Soon plant pots and other garden ornaments were being hurled through the windows of the hotel.

The familiar sound of police sirens could soon be heard and that was the signal for us to disperse and make our way to a pub that was the planned meeting place. When the police did arrive, Motherwell were ordered out of their hotel and returned home, cutting their break short. The Fat Controller and his mates made excuses and followed suit, as they must have known they were going to be next to get attacked.

With Motherwell out of the way, our attention turned to enjoying ourselves and getting laid. It wasn't too hard to pick up a bird and soon Big Tonto and me got hold of a couple of girls from Belfast. They were quite rough, but well up for it. We decided to take them back to our digs and left the club. Tonto had the keys to the dorm-like room, which six or seven of us were sharing. He got there just before me and locked himself in with his bird while I went to the bar for a drink.

I thought I would give him a bit of privacy and didn't go back to the room for about half an hour. However, he had other plans and had put a wardrobe against the door. Nobody else could get in. By this time, everyone else was arriving back at the digs. Some of them had birds and wanted to get back into the room.

Big Tonto was having none of it and, no matter how hard we tried, he wouldn't let us in. I don't think he even shagged the bird. Knowing him, he probably fell asleep. The rest of us had to double up in the other rooms. The rest of the weekend was good fun and had helped to strengthen the bond that was growing among the hardcore of the Crew.

A few weeks after Blackpool, we were to meet the Hibs boys again, this time in the centre circle of the pitch at Easter Road. Hibs by this time had established themselves as the mob everyone wanted to turn over. They were widely regarded as the top firm in Scotland. Not only did they have numbers, but they also had a lot of game boys and seemed to be very organised.

Celtic had a big Crew and we had claimed a couple of notable scalps in the run-up to the game against Hibs. We had played them in a Cup game at Easter Road on a Wednesday night and had come back to Glasgow with a feather in our caps, as only 25 of us had travelled through and put up a good show without being turned over. This resulted in us managing to attract a far larger Crew for a League game in November 1987.

There was a rumour going about the Crew that somebody had brought a CS gas grenade with them back from a TA training camp and would be taking it to Easter Road. We met at Queen Street Station on the Saturday morning and awaited the arrival of our various mobs. It soon became clear that the rumour regarding the gas was indeed true.

This was getting a bit heavy and we had to decide how

best to deal with it. Those of us who had been involved with the serious assault at Hearts were naturally uneasy about being caught up in another serious incident. We decided to send the Babes and the bulk of the Crew through on the football special, while some of us would get a service train and meet them there. The journey to Easter Road was quite uneventful for those of us who had travelled behind the bulk of the Crew.

However, when we got to the small railway bridge that leads to the away end, we were met by a small group of Hibs. One of them picked me out and asked for a square go. I eyed him up and fancied my chances, as he looked younger and smaller than me. I threw a punch in his direction which didn't connect as he was much quicker than me and simply ducked to the side, while unleashing a volley of punches with the accuracy of a trained fighter. I was glad when an undercover cop came over and stopped the fight. He warned us about our behaviour and told me to pick on someone my own size. Considering the black eye that was beginning to appear on my face, it was quite ironic!

We made our way to the stadium and took our place on the uncovered terrace behind one of the goals. Most of our Crew were standing beside the fence which separated the away fans from the home support. Hibs were gathered under the enclosure which ran one length of the pitch facing the main stand. The first half passed without major incident with only a couple of coins being thrown at one another.

However, early in the second half, we were told that somebody was going to throw the grenade. A few of us stood away from the main group. They began to bounce up and down singing some ridiculous song, when all of a sudden there was a loud bang coming from the direction of the Hibs end.

A large cloud of smoke began to rise and spread out, engulfing all those who were in the shed. People began to clamber over the fence and on to the pitch, choking and spluttering with tears streaming down their faces. The Celtic lads were jumping up and down in jubilation, unaware of the large cloud of smoke heading towards us.

Soon we were piling over the fence and on to the pitch to escape the noxious gas. Hibs had gathered in the middle of the pitch preparing to attack us once we were over the fence. The scene was chaotic with paramedics and police running all over the place attending to the injured.

Our Crew gathered in the goalmouth where we tried to regain our composure. There were a lot of lads suffering the effects of the gas. As we grouped up, the Celtic support that were in the terrace behind the goal began to vent their anger towards us. There was the usual chant of 'Casuals, Casuals, get to fuck', as a hail of coins rained down on those of us in the goalmouth. In an effort to escape the barrage of missiles, a lot of our lads surged forward in the direction of the 50 or so CCS who had assembled near the halfway line. This seemed to take the Hibs firm by surprise. They must have thought that we were charging them, but in reality we were running away from the constant stream of coins raining down on us. However, intentional or not, we managed to run the CCS towards the other side of the pitch. The police mounted division had now entered the stadium and focused their attention on escorting our Crew out of the ground.

Once outside, we were met by a small group of the Hibs Baby Crew who attempted to attack us. The mounted police again intervened, driving back the young Hibs boys. Our Crew had numbered a couple of hundred when we were assembled in the goalmouth, but now, as we stood outside the stadium, it was very noticeable that a lot of lads had deserted us. It was clear that many of the Crew had decided they didn't fancy the walk back to the train station in the knowledge that the CCS would be hell-bent on revenge. I witnessed some boys buying Celtic scarves from the vendors, while others had managed to get taxis or had slipped away on to the terrace to mingle with the Celtic support. This left about 50 or 60 of us to face running the gauntlet from the stadium to the safety of Waverly Station.

As we turned on to Easter Road, we could see groups standing at every corner and pub door. We tried to stick together as a unit, but this was easier said than done. It was now dark, which made it difficult to keep an eye on everyone in the Crew. The CCS were attacking us from all directions and we were taking one hell of a beating. The police offered no respite, as they seemed to be turning a blind eye, probably thinking that we deserved a good kicking. That journey back to the train station is the most frightening experience that I have ever suffered in over 20 years of my involvement in football hooliganism. When we eventually reached the relative safety of the train station, the Crew resembled an army returning from the trenches. There were boys with black eyes, cuts to the head, ripped clothes and even one who only had one trainer, having lost the other shoe in the chaos caused when the gas blew back on to us.

The mood amongst the Crew on the journey back to Glasgow was very sombre. There had been rumours circulating which claimed some spectators had actually died as a result of our actions that day. When we arrived in Glasgow, a lot of the lads hurried to the news vendors who were selling the evening paper to buy a copy. The Saturday edition of the *Glasgow Evening Times* usually only carried the day's football results with a brief match report. However, on this occasion, the sports headlines were replaced by the terrifying images of the day's events at Easter Road. The paper did, however, allay our fears concerning fatalities. Thankfully, there were no reports of anyone being too seriously injured, although several people were being kept in hospital for observation, with some older fans suffering from respiratory problems as a result of inhaling the gas.

The next couple of days were very tense for all of us associated with the Celtic Soccer Crew. The biggest daily paper in Scotland, the *Daily Record*, had urged the so-called decent Celtic supporters to contact a confidential hotline if they had any information on any Celtic Casuals. It wasn't long before the Edinburgh Police were knocking on the doors of known and not so well-known Celtic Soccer Crew members. The police were certainly putting the pressure on and were even turning up at some of the lads' workplaces, which jeopardised their jobs, as their bosses weren't too impressed when they found out their employees were also football hooligans.

When the chap came to my door, it wasn't unexpected. Thankfully for me, my dad was in the house at the time and basically cut the interrogation short when the coppers began to apply the good cop, bad cop routine. My dad intervened when the bad cop threatened to take me to St Leonard's Police Station in Edinburgh for further questioning. My dad asked the officers if they had a warrant. When they replied, 'No, but we can get one,' my dad told them to leave the house and not to return unless they had a warrant. The two coppers reluctantly made their exit, but not before they threatened me by saying I was a prime suspect and not out of the woods yet. My dad then turned his anger towards me. Although he had been absolutely superb in dealing with the police, it didn't mean he wasn't pissed off with me, especially after all the promises I had made when I got out of prison only a few months earlier. I had said I wouldn't go back to the football and that I was finished with the CSC.

Nevertheless, that was the last visit that I received from the police regarding the CS gas incident. Frank, on the other hand, wasn't as fortunate; he was one of the first to be arrested and this time his slick Edinburgh lawyer was unable to pull any stunts, meaning he would spend 16 weeks on remand in prison to await yet another High Court appearance, his second in the space of nine months. There were about another six or seven people arrested, two of whom were twin brothers who had foolishly called the *Daily Record* hotline. Not only were they stupid in calling the newspaper, but unbelievably they did so from a payphone in their local general store. A shop assistant or customer overheard their conversation and called the police as soon as the pair had left the shop. The two brothers were arrested shortly afterwards and joined the others for the High Court trial, which was held in Edinburgh in February 1988. The trial lasted a few days before a plea bargain was struck, resulting in the lad who supplied the canister of gas and the person who actually threw it receiving substantial sentences while the others in the dock, Frank and the twins included, walked free.

CHAPTER 5

The centenary season was an eventful year for Celtic, both on and off the pitch. The team showed a tremendous will to win and were rewarded for their efforts with the League and Scottish Cup making their way to Celtic Park.

The Celtic Soccer Crew can also look back on that season as a milestone. Following the Hibs game, a lot of lads called it a day due to the publicity and fear of losing their jobs. We did, however, attract interest from some lads from down south. One mob which came up in numbers was Wrexham, who hated the English and the Huns as much as us. Other lads from the Northampton area made trips north. They consisted of exiled Celtic fans, Spurs Casuals and a couple of Man United boys. A lot of us had reservations regarding other mobs trying to muscle in, but we needn't have worried as all the lads were spot on.

A large crowd had come up for the Cup Final against Dundee United. Such was the confidence we had for a Celtic victory, we planned a party in a nightclub for after the game. The match itself passed without incident, as United fans were more intent on coming to Hampden and enjoying the occasion.

Celtic won the match 2–1, after suffering a scare by being a goal down until the last 10 minutes. Our mob enjoyed the celebrations with the Celtic fans and eventually made our way to the city centre without any trouble. After a few drinks, a lot of lads went home to get changed and we arranged to meet later at a bar before going to the party. We met at the agreed time, everyone looking smart and in a jovial mood. The last thing we were looking for was trouble.

We had booked a hall in a nightclub close to Queen Street Station. The rest of the club was open to the public, which meant our crowd was sharing the toilets with the paying public. The party was in full swing and most of the Celtic boys were oblivious to any trouble that was taking place.

The Wrexham and English boys had been involved in a few scraps in the toilets. A few lads went to investigate and we soon learned that a mob of Rangers had gathered in the other hall along with a crowd from Possil – a tough scheme in the north of Glasgow. We decided to confront them and started to make our way out of the hall when we were stopped by a wall of CS gas and a couple of guys wielding blades.

We were taken by surprise and didn't stand a chance. One of the Wrexham boys, probably caught unawares, was an easy target and got slashed quite badly down his back. None of our crowd had any weapons and some of the lads, along with the girls, headed for the emergency exits. However, the Wrexham boys and some Celtic lads armed themselves with chairs and bottles and steamed into the crowd who were attacking us. The bouncers quickly appeared and sheltered the Possil mob, allowing them to escape before we could catch them and also before the police arrived.

The party came to an abrupt end with the police wanting statements. Most people claimed to be in the toilet or the dance floor at the time of the fight, thus giving them no information to work on. We were gutted at being turned over and vowed revenge.

It was now March 1989 and Celtic had just recorded a memorable victory against Rangers at Celtic Park. The Northampton boys had come up in a minibus for the weekend with most of them booking into a hotel and a couple staying at Frank's mother's house. Frank was now living down south following his experiences of two High Court trials in the space of one year. He wanted to get away from the temptation that he faced every time Celtic played and there was trouble. I suppose escaping was to him the equivalent of a junkie booking into a drying-out clinic!

After the match, I had planned to go home and get

changed, but there had been trouble with Rangers at the Barras and we stayed together as a mob in the town. A couple of the Spurs boys got lifted, probably for doing things that they get away with every week in London, not knowing that the Glasgow Police are not as lenient as their counterparts in England. I have travelled all over Britain and Europe and have yet to meet a police force as intolerable as the one in Glasgow.

The night was getting on and I decided to go the hotel where I could borrow clothes that would be suitable for a night out clubbing. I acquired a pair of jeans and shoes from Frank's brother and was given a T-shirt from one of the English boys. What I didn't know was that it was one of the Spurs boys who was jailed and he had paid about £70 for it that day.

We went to a few pubs and met up with the others, before eventually making our way to a nightclub. At this time, Glasgow's riverside was awash with clubs. We decided to head for Panama Jacks, which was near the suspension bridge. Some younger lads got a knock-back for wearing trainers and the like. It meant that only about 10–15 of us got in the club. We were only in the place a short time when we became aware of a large crowd of Rangers beginning to surround us.

I stepped out on to the dance floor to see if I could find more of our mob. All of a sudden, one of their mob ran towards me brandishing a barstool. I didn't have time to react and felt the full force of the stool connect with the bridge of my nose. One of our mob had a can of CS gas with him and began to spray it. Soon all hell broke out, as people began choking and screaming while stampeding towards the exits. I was suffering from the effects of the gas and made my way to the toilets to rinse my face and eyes. This allowed the majority of the clubbers time to leave the club, giving us time to regroup. I immediately took the tin of gas from the guy who'd sprayed it and led the Crew outside.

We were soon met with a crowd running towards us. I ran into them spraying the gas, before realising it was a crowd of Celtic Babes who had been drinking at the bandstand close by. Once they had recovered from the gas, we made our way up to the main road to confront the Rangers mob. They were spread across the road about 30 yards in front of us. I ran towards them with the can of gas in my hand outstretched in front of me. As I got close, I noticed the guy directly in front of me was armed with a large blade. I attempted to spray the gas towards him, but to my horror the can was empty. I quickly turned to back off but felt a blow to my thigh. I made my way back to my mates who had chased the rest of the Rangers lads. I felt dizzy and could hear a squelching sound coming from my shoes.

I was in shock and unaware of what had happened. My mates were trying to reassure me and keep me calm. My trousers had turned a dark crimson and were soaked in blood. Still I asked what was wrong. Everyone was telling me I was OK until my mate Skelly, who is not the brightest, told me I'd been stabbed.

I immediately collapsed in a heap and was quickly bundled into a taxi and taken to the Royal Infirmary where doctors carried out an emergency operation to repair a severed artery. I remember coming round the next day wired to all sorts of machines and monitors. The most frightening part was watching the heart monitor and thinking, If that stop bleeping and the lines go straight, then it's curtains.

The remainder of the 1988–89 season passed without any major incident. It was, however, a significant year in the history of Scottish football. Celtic had enjoyed a fair degree of success throughout the 80s and the Board seemed unfazed by the arrival of Souness at Ibrox and the Murray millions he had at his disposal. The League title was surrendered with alarming ease, but we had an opportunity to salvage something from the season and also prevent Rangers from winning the domestic treble.

Celtic had battled their way through to the Scottish Cup Final for a showdown against their biggest rivals. The CSC was in some disarray at this time and found it difficult to pull a decent mob. The usual lads did meet up and we made our way to Hampden without any great enthusiasm, not really expecting to win.

There was a rumour going about that Celtic had made a major signing and he would be introduced to the crowd before the game. Most Celtic fans had dismissed this as a stunt by the Board to disguise the fact that they were unwilling to match the millions being spent by Rangers.

The Celtic fans congregated on the vast open terrace while the Huns took their traditional positions below the covered terrace. The usual exchange of songs and insults was building up with the Rangers fans drowning out the Celtic songs, mainly as they had the benefit of a roof above their heads.

However, they were shocked into silence when the Celtic players came out to warm up. There was a familiar figure standing on the touchline beside Billy McNeil, who was our manager at the time. The Celtic fans went mental and you would have thought we were the team who were going for the treble. To all of our amazement, Maurice Johnston, who had been a sensation with Celtic, was being introduced to all the players. This was being hailed as a brilliant coup and lifted the team as well as the fans. The players seemed to find an extra yard and were first to every ball, forcing Rangers into mistakes which led to Joe Miller pouncing on a slack pass back and scoring the winner for Celtic.

The celebrations that followed the final whistle were pretty wild, even by our standards. By the time our mob had left the stadium, all the Rangers fans had long gone, meaning we wouldn't have a chance to get a fight with the ICF.

A couple of us decided to go with a group of Celtic

lads who lived in Pollokshields, which wasn't too far from Hampden. We were in a good mood and singing as we made our way to the pub. Uhoomagoo was singing a song about Mo Johnston, praising him. We soon attracted the attention of a couple of cops in a van, who approached us and told us to be quiet or we would be lifted. Uhoomagoo didn't listen and burst into another chorus of 'Mo, Mo, Super Mo'. The coppers never gave him a second chance and jailed him.

But that was not the end of the saga surrounding Mo Johnston. For the next few weeks, every newspaper carried stories about Mo Johnston. It soon became clear that he hadn't actually signed for Celtic, but had merely shook hands with the manager with the understanding he would sign before the new season began.

As the summer break went on, the story faded out of the papers. On the morning of 10 July 1989, the Glasgow rumour factory was working overtime. Word was going about saying Johnston had signed for Rangers. I didn't believe it for one minute. After all, he was a Catholic and Rangers didn't sign Catholics.

I was on my tea break at work when a newsflash was announced on the radio. My workmates and I gathered around the radio and began looking at each other in disbelief as the broadcaster confirmed Johnston had signed for the Huns. A lot of guys I worked with were Rangers fans and they were more upset than the Celtic boys.

It was quite clear there wasn't going to be much

work being done, so the boss let us knock off. Most of us made our way to a pub which was already packed with stunned fans from both halves of the Old Firm. The lunchtime news bulletin was fast approaching and all eyes were focused on the giant screen and the various televisions situated around the bar.

There were pictures of Rangers fans burning their scarves and season tickets outside the doors of Ibrox Stadium and vowing never to set foot back in the ground. The rivalry between the Old Firm is legendary, but this time they were united in grief. Celtic fans felt betrayed and couldn't understand how somebody who was a staunch Celtic fan could sign for Rangers. On the other hand, the Rangers fans were trying to understand how a Protestant club could break tradition in such a manner.

Graeme Souness must have known the risk he'd taken could have finished him as a manager, but he seemed to be enjoying the commotion he had stirred up. For the next couple of weeks, nobody talked about anything else. Johnston himself had to move to the east coast to live, as he couldn't walk the streets of Glasgow without fear of being attacked.

The new season was soon upon us and the effects of the signing seemed to stir a lot of lads into going back to football with the CSC. One familiar face was missing, however. Uhoomagoo was to stand trial for his breach and was to find himself making the newspapers.

The trial took place in Glasgow District Court, where he was subsequently found guilty and remanded in custody. I remember the headline in Glasgow's *Evening Times* which announced 'Celtic fan suffers double heartache'. It went on to say, 'Not only did his hero join Rangers but the judge showed little sympathy in imposing a three-week remand.' He was, however, soon to receive some company during his stay in Longrigend following Celtic's visit to Love Street near the beginning of the season.

The police by this point were cracking down on football violence, making it almost impossible for our Crew to travel on football specials. This resulted in us wanting to take the more dangerous route to Paisley by bus, which travelled along Paisley Road, past Ibrox Stadium and a large number of pubs frequented by the ICF and hardened loyalists.

We met as usual in the Country Corner and had quite a good mob that was willing to run the gauntlet along Paisley Road. We were just about to leave when somebody came running into the pub to say a mob of Rangers were approaching. There were about 50 of us and, looking around, I could tell it was a good crowd of experienced lads you could rely on.

We left the pub to confront the ICF, whose mob numbered over 100. We ran at them but their mob stood firm, resulting in some of our boys running off. We looked as if we were going to get turned over when all of a sudden a crowd of about 30 Shirties came running round a corner behind Rangers. This was the break we needed, and now that numbers were even we steamed in with added confidence. It's hard to say who was winning when the police came up, but it was one of the best toe-to-toes I ever had with Rangers.

The police arrived in force, accompanied by the mounties. Both mobs scattered, with Rangers heading towards Ibrox and us into the city centre. With the one-way system that exists in Glasgow, it was quite easy to escape arrest as the volume of traffic prevented police vehicles from following us. We all met up in a pub in the city centre and decided it would be too risky to get a bus to Paisley, not only because of the Rangers fans and ICF baying for our blood but also because of the amount of coppers down there.

A small group of us had tickets for the match and decided to risk taking a train. There were only about 12 of us and we managed to get a train without too much hassle. We got off at Gilmour Street and made our way to a pub to meet some Celtic who lived in that area. Once we met up, our crowd numbered about 40 and we decided to have a look for St Mirren, who were rumoured to be in some pool hall.

As we approached the club, we were met by a crowd of St Mirren Casuals who were armed with cues. We were quite wary as we had no weapons, but that soon changed. To my amazement, St Mirren ran at us and, as they got near, began throwing their cues at us. This gave us the chance to pick up the cues and steam in. We chased them back into the club where they held the doors closed. A few windows were broken and a couple of cars in the car park were smashed up. We retreated before the police arrived and ditched the cues.

The coppers soon caught up with us and they had the barman from the club in a car to pick out those responsible. As usual, I was picked out along with three others – one of whom had a speech impediment and couldn't communicate with the police. At first they thought he was taking the piss but quickly released him when they realised he was genuine.

That guy was Big Peter, who was one of the nicest and boldest guys ever to run with Celtic. Sadly, he is no longer with us but hopefully his name will live on forever with this tribute that loads of people asked me to pay him.

The rest of us were taken to Mill Street Police Station and charged with the usual breach. The desk sergeant was decent enough and told us we would get out if our addresses checked out. A couple of hours later, the hatch on the door of my cell was opened and I was told by the officer that my dad had told them I didn't stay with him. This meant that I would appear in court on the Monday. I planned to plead guilty as I thought I would get a fine.

On the Monday, my lawyer told me my dad was in court and would verify my address. She said he was trying to teach me a lesson by letting me stew all weekend. My lawyer told me to plead not guilty as the Fiscal was not opposing bail.

I entered the dock with confidence and expected the proceedings to be a formality. My lawyer tendered my plea of not guilty and asked for bail. The Fiscal said there was no objection and asked for a trial date to be fixed. However, the judge wanted to know why my dad hadn't verified my address on the Saturday. My dad stood up in court and explained he wanted to teach me a lesson. The judge said he understood, but added that if my own father felt I needed a lesson then I didn't merit being granted bail and overturned the decision. I was remanded in custody for five weeks.

I was absolutely gutted and tried to change my plea to guilty, which the Fiscal declined because I had already pleaded not guilty, thus raising a doubt regarding my guilt. I was taken to Longrigend Remand Centre and put into the same wing as Uhoomagoo and a couple of other Celtic boys.

When I returned to court, I pleaded guilty and was fined a paltry £100, which I think was ironic considering my crime cost the taxpayer thousands because of the five weeks I spent on remand.

While I was in prison awaiting trial, I received visits from my dad. He made it clear that, although he hadn't expected me to be sent to prison, he hoped that it would give me time to reflect on which path I wanted to choose for my future. He said he had phoned my sister and she had agreed to let me stay with her when

I got out. She lived in Garelochhead, which is a small village on the Clyde coast about eight miles from Helensburgh. Anne was now married and had a baby daughter. She had met her husband, who was a St Mirren fan, at a Scotland match at Hampden when she was about 16, which was around the same time that I was placed into care.

Even though I was out of the family home at this point, home life had still been very chaotic and unbearable for my brother and sister. Andrew put all of his frustrations and energy into his religion and became a fully fledged Jehovah's Witness. As I see it, this was his way of escaping from the harsh realities of his everyday life, going from one extreme to another, which he is still committed to today. Anne found a more conventional escape by falling in love and moving out of the family home at 16. She did, however, wait until the day of her 18th birthday to get married.

Anne had told me that she would try to get me a start as a labourer with the building firm that she worked for as a secretary. A few days after getting out of prison, I said my goodbyes to my dad and life in the city to move down the coast to live with my sister and her husband. As promised, my sister got me a start with her company. I was now a general labourer working on a site at Faslane, which is the Clyde submarine base and home to Britain's nuclear fleet. At first, I found it hard going, but soon got used to the hard graft, made easier by the fantastic wages that I was earning. I was only 20 years old, single and had no commitments, but I was taking home the same pay as guys who had families and mortgages. I was clearing between £200 and £250 every week, of which I handed my sister £30 for my keep. Things were going really well for me. For the first time in my life, I had money to spend.

I had been working for about six months by the time the festive season was upon us. The company had arranged a Christmas night out with all costs paid for, including a meal and free bar. The night out was planned for the Friday before my 21st birthday. I was the only person in the 60- or 70-strong party who didn't take advantage of the alcohol on offer at the free bar, as I had agreed to work that weekend in order to make up the hours that I had asked to take off the following week for my birthday. So, while everyone around me indulged in the free-flowing booze, I stuck stringently to soft drinks.

As the night wore on, one idiot in particular began to become unruly and was trying to pick fights with the younger people at our table. He turned his drunken abuse towards me, saying, 'All you Glaswegians think you are tough nuts.'

I chose to ignore him, which seemed to incense him even more and his ranting became louder. I told him to calm down and stop being a dickhead. All of a sudden, he cleared his throat and directed phlegm-filled spittle towards me. It missed, but, as I was telling him again to calm down, he cleared his throat for a second time before letting fly in my direction, with some success this time. I was now incandescent with rage and instinctively grabbed hold of my glass, which contained no more than orange juice. He was attempting to clear his throat for the third time when a red mist descended over me, resulting in the glass becoming embedded in the disgusting bully's face.

All hell broke loose with the bosses jumping from their chairs to intervene in the fracas that had now developed. I was ushered out of a side door, while the drunken bully was playing the innocent victim and lapping up all the concerned attention he was receiving. Before long, a couple of ambulances arrived, and I went to hospital in one, while the hapless victim went in the other. I received about 20 stitches to my right palm. I didn't know much about the other guy's injuries. I reported for work the next morning, despite my hand being heavily bandaged. I was met at the gatehouse by one of my bosses and the local police. The bully's father, who happened to be a military policeman at the base, was also there. I was asked to hand over my security pass and was sacked on the spot. The bully's father offered me his hand and, surprisingly, he apologised for his son's behaviour. He said that his injuries were mainly superficial and he wouldn't be pressing any charges.

I would never condone the use of glasses in a fight and I am not trying to justify my actions that night, even though it was done under extreme provocation. I am, however, thankful that it was only my job and not my liberty I lost, as I realise I could have been in serious trouble if the glass had done more damage.

CHAPTER 6

After getting the sack, I went back to Castlemilk to stay at my dad's house. However, we were forever fighting and falling out. I understand now the pressure and grief I was bringing to the house and the hassle I caused for my dad. I decided to leave Glasgow and try to find work in London. A few Celtic boys were already down south and were willing to let me stay with them. I quickly found work but I couldn't settle and returned to Glasgow a couple of weeks before the Scottish Cup Final of 1990.

Rangers had won the League again and it was left to Celtic and Aberdeen to fight it out in the Scottish Cup Final. The Aberdeen Casuals had come to Glasgow in big numbers, most of them arriving on the Friday. A crowd of Celtic were out on the Friday night and came across a crowd of ASC in a pub. Aberdeen have always been a good mob and command a degree of respect from other firms. The crowd in the pub were older boys, who appeared to be among their top boys. They weren't looking for trouble that night and they didn't want to blow it for the big day. The Celtic boys could have taken a liberty, but that's not our style. We knew it would be better to arrange something for the next day.

They said the rest of their mob had arranged to meet in Sylvesters at opening time. A meeting was set up for the next day. A lot of phone calls were made that night, resulting in Celtic attracting one of the biggest mobs we had had for years. We arranged to meet in various pubs surrounding George Square and close to Sylvesters.

A couple of younger boys sat in the burger bar in Queen Street Station to watch for the rest of Aberdeen coming off the train. At about 12.30pm, the word was going round that the Aberdeen train was about to arrive. The pubs emptied and our mob made our way into George Square from all directions.

The timing was perfect, as Aberdeen were starting to head towards the square, oblivious to the ambush that awaited them. Even though Celtic had been split up into different mobs in the pubs, everybody knew what was expected of them. As Aberdeen entered George Square, a bang was heard as somebody from our Crew fired a flare towards them. This was the signal for everyone to charge in. Aberdeen ran back into the station and the police surrounded the entrances to prevent us getting in. We retreated to a pub on Miller Street, which was downstairs in a hotel and large enough for everyone to get in. We knew that it wasn't Aberdeen's main boys we had done and planned to attack their pub quickly while there was still a lot of confusion following the attack in George Square. We knew that the police would be concentrating on escorting the mob in the station, believing they were the majority of Aberdeen. We sent a couple of older lads along to Sylvesters to see how many Aberdeen were in there. It wasn't long before we got the word back that there was a healthy firm of Aberdeen's main mob in the pub.

We left the hotel bar and made the short journey along Ingram Street towards Sylvesters. We must have had a mob of about 200, who were already hyped up as a result of the events in George Square. As we got near the pub, Aberdeen attempted to steam out the door towards us. However, only a couple could get out at a time and they found themselves in amongst hundreds of Celtic. A stand-off developed, as Aberdeen were reluctant to steam out and the Celtic boys were reluctant to charge up the steps into a glass or bottle.

One of our mob was waving about a large traffic cone and somebody suggested he should throw it through the windows of the pub. The big plate window was soon smashed, resulting in some of the boys charging into the pub through the hole that the cone had created. The fight mostly consisted of the two mobs exchanging bottles, chairs and tables. It wasn't really a fist fight. After what seemed like ages, sirens could be heard heading in our direction. Our mob began to disperse in all directions to make their way to our meeting point.

Some of our lads had to come back out of the pub through the window. All but one got out unscathed. Big Ped, who was one of the first in, was last to leave. On exiting, he kicked out the glass that was still in the frame. Somebody shouted to him to watch out, but it was too late. A large piece of glass fell from the top of the frame, stabbing Ped in the stomach.

I ran over to help him and knew he needed to get to a hospital as quick as possible. There was an ambulance sitting in traffic someway along the road. I grabbed Ped by the arm and hurried him along to the ambulance. I banged on the window and asked if they could take Ped to hospital. They said they were only allowed to respond to calls. The cops were on the scene by this point and one of them radioed control, who gave permission for them to take Ped to hospital.

The cop knew we had been involved in the fight and asked us what happened. I said we were in the pub waiting to go to the match when a riot broke out. He asked us to produce tickets to prove our story. I thought the game was up when, to my surprise, Ped took a match ticket out of his pocket.

The cop gave us the benefit of the doubt but added he would be following the ambulance to hospital where he would get full statements from us. When he left the ambulance, I asked the paramedic if I had to go to hospital. He said I could leave Ped in their care if I wanted.

Before leaving the ambulance, I realised that Ped wouldn't be needing his ticket. So, in the true traditions of the Dirty Bastard Club, I asked him to give it to me. I then wished him all the best and made my way to find the others.

The streets were awash with coppers stopping anybody who they suspected of being involved in the fight. I decided to mingle with the Saturday shoppers and head towards St Enoch Square, where I knew some of the Crew would be.

I met about 15–20 who had gathered in one of the pubs. I soon learned that the main mob was in an escort heading towards Hampden Park. We decided to bide our time and wait for everything to settle down before boarding a bus to the game. We met up with the rest of the boys and arranged a meeting point for after the match. There were loads of people looking for tickets and offering crazy amounts of money. I decided to sell Ped's ticket and go to the pub with a couple of boys to watch the football.

The match itself was a dull affair with both teams more frightened of losing than anything else. This resulted in a penalty shoot-out to decide the outcome.

Both teams missed penalties early on – meaning that after five each they were still level. It was now sudden death with the scores tied at 8–8. Anton Rogan stepped up to take our next kick. The Celtic fans in the pub seemed to sense he would miss. A lot of us couldn't bear to watch and went to the toilet to await the cheers.

However, we soon knew that our worst fears had been confirmed with the sound of breaking glass, as people threw their tumblers at the big screen in disgust. We left the pub just as Aberdeen scored the deciding penalty. There was about half-a-dozen of us making our way to Hampden to meet up with the others. We got to the garage just outside the Celtic end where we met up with about 40 other Celtic.

The police quickly moved us on, thus preventing the rest of the mob joining us. We had to decide if the mob we were in was good enough to have a go at Aberdeen. There were a few people saying we should head into the town but more wanted to go up towards Cathcart Road where we could get Aberdeen. We managed to slip the police escort by turning up a street that ran alongside Holyrood School. We regrouped just before the junction with Cathcart Road and could see hundreds of Aberdeen scarfers walking along – oblivious to the 50 or so of us lurking in the side street. We knew we would be vastly outnumbered but would have the element of surprise in our favour.

A couple of younger boys were sent to the corner

and told to signal when they saw the Aberdeen mob. A few boys armed themselves with posts they acquired by ripping down a fence which surrounded one of the many neat gardens that made up this quiet neighbourhood.

We didn't have long to wait before the signal was given that Aberdeen were approaching. We ran out on Cathcart Road just in front of them, taking them by complete surprise. We were gaining the upper hand when they realised there weren't that many of us. They charged into us but to our credit all our boys stood their ground. Again, the sound of police sirens brought a halt to proceedings.

An Aberdeen lad, who I'd been going toe-to-toe with, was arrested. He was put in a police minibus which was just ahead of me. He was shouting and pointing in my direction claiming I had a knife on me. Two coppers grabbed me and asked to search me. I had no reason to refuse, as I have never carried a knife at a football match. The search didn't take long and, on finding nothing, they told me I could go. However, just before I was out of harm's way, another cop in the van said he knew me and they were to lift me for a breach. I was livid and as the coppers put me the van I kicked out at the Aberdeen grass, getting him in the face. I was quickly restrained and taken to the local police station to be charged.

The place was heaving with a queue leading out to the corridor. I noticed a couple of Celtic boys that I knew and began to shout at them about the Aberdeen lad grassing. At the same time, I was kicking out wildly in the grass's direction. The two Celtic boys, Jambo and Paulso, quite rightly blanked me, pretending they didn't know who I was. I was bundled into a side room and told to calm down. The two arresting officers were actually quite decent and said I would most likely get out if my address checked out and I behaved myself.

Once I was charged, I was put in a cell alongside about six other Celtic boys. I soon learned that they had been involved in a fight with Aberdeen further along the road beside Hampden Park. Uhoomagoo was among the others lifted and his was the first name to be called. He asked everyone if we needed any calls to be made as he gathered his belongings and said his goodbyes. However, his mood soon changed as the turnkey told him he was being moved to another cell as he had a warrant outstanding. The rest of us were out later that evening and headed into town for a pint with the rest of the boys and to recount the day's events. We also promised to go to court to see how Uhoomagoo would get on.

Uhoomagoo appeared at court on the Monday where he pleaded guilty in the hope of receiving a fine. However, the judge asked for background reports and deferred sentence for three weeks, releasing him on bail in the process.

The season was now over and all talk was about travelling to Italy for the World Cup Finals. Gumsy,

Mick, wee Gary and about five others had booked a trip to Yugoslavia, which was about five hours from Genoa, but much cheaper.

I planned with Uhoomagoo to travel with a couple of boys who now lived in London. The idea was to go down to the Smoke and work for a few weeks to raise the money that we would need. We'd planned to leave Glasgow on the day of Uhoo's court case but, in the true spirit of the CSC planning, we hadn't anticipated the outcome of the court appearance.

The social work reports were encouraging and his lawyer expected Uhoo to be dealt with by way of a fine. The judge on the bench that day was the same one who had dealt with the infamous Mo Johnston incident concerning Uhoo. He asked if he was planning on going to Italy. Uhoo replied he would like to but couldn't afford it. The judge replied that he valued Scotland's reputation abroad and wouldn't like to see it tarnished by hooligans passing themselves off as football fans. He sentenced Uhoo to 60 days' imprisonment, thus ensuring he wouldn't be going.

I decided to go to London anyway, telling my father that I had a job lined up and I wanted to get away from Glasgow and put an end to my involvement with the Crew. I assured him I had no intention of travelling to Italy.

I got a job within a couple of days of arriving in London. However, it soon became clear that the cost of living in the English capital would leave me very little out of my wages and certainly not enough to go to Italy for a few weeks. We gave up all hope when Frank came home one Thursday night and said he was being paid off.

Tonto and his girlfriend were leaving on the Saturday from London and were trying everything possible to help Frank and me – but we accepted we had no chance. I was getting ready to go to work on the Friday morning when Frank came into my room yelling excitedly and waving an envelope wildly above his head. I asked him what all the fuss was about and managed to work out, amongst the hysteria, that Frank had received an Access credit card.

I said it was too late to make any arrangements but he had an answer for everything and soon I was caught up in the excitement. I called my boss and told him I had to go to Glasgow immediately for a funeral and asked him to make up my wages to collect before lunch. We then sat down and talked about the things we would need to do before we could go.

The pair of us didn't even have a passport, so this became the first priority along with calling our landlord and seeing if they would come to an arrangement regarding the month's rent that was due. They eventually agreed to accept a post-dated cheque, which I happily handed over using an old chequebook from a long overdrawn account in Glasgow. We then set off to the West End to purchase train tickets and passports. Frank had no bother getting a one-year passport, but I didn't have enough identification on me. We then moved on to get the train tickets. Frank got himself a Euro star one, which gave him unlimited travel throughout Europe for one month. Again, I encountered problems. Because I didn't have a passport, they couldn't issue me with one of these tickets. We now faced a race against time, as I had to go back to our flat to get more ID and purchase a passport before 5.30pm.

It was clear that there wasn't enough time to get back to the flat and then into the West End again. I decided that I didn't want to chance buying a Euro star ticket and not being able to get a passport. It would've been a lot of cash down the tubes. Tonto suggested I get the cheapest ticket to Italy with the view of upgrading it once, and if, I got there.

I managed to buy a one-way ticket to Genoa for about £50. It was by now mid-afternoon and the race was on to get home and get enough ID. Eventually, I was issued with a passport about half-an-hour from closing time – owing mostly to the fact that the counter clerk was Spurs and he was also going to Italy.

We set off the next morning, heading for Dover to catch a lunchtime crossing to Calais. There were only four of us in our group, consisting of myself, Frank, Tonto and his girlfriend. We didn't anticipate any hassle from the police but we took the precaution of wearing Celtic hats and Scotland tops to distinguish us from the hordes of English who were travelling.

We got through the barriers at Dover without any problem, and made our way on to the boat and into one of the bars.

The boat itself was surprisingly quiet with only a handful of other supporters aboard. There was one Scotland fan in particular who looked to be alone, which led to us asking him to join our company for a drink. He was a man in his fifties, resplendent in a blazer sporting a Scotland badge with a pressed shirt and tie. We soon learned that his name was Gordon and he had lived in England for a while but was still passionately Scottish. He was travelling to Genoa but had no arrangements made. He then joined up with us for an unforgettable journey.

By the time we arrived in Calais, we were all a little drunk, mainly because we hadn't realised that mainland Europe was an hour ahead of Britain. We still had a table full of drinks when the boat began to dock. Being typical Glaswegians, we finished our drinks before disembarking. We quickly sobered up when we saw what was awaiting us in France.

There were loads of police who were waving through the majority of people, giving us no reason to worry, when all of a sudden we were approached by British coppers and told to follow them into a room, which had a number of tables with pictures behind them showing various mobs from all over Britain.

We were led to a table which had 'Scotland' written on the wall behind it and asked various questions about our previous convictions and involvement with Celtic. Gordon was told he could go but he insisted he was with us, which I think threw the coppers. One by one, everyone was told they could leave... bar me. They wanted to know why I was travelling on a one-way ticket and if I was expecting to be deported. Eventually, after about 20 minutes, and a check for warrants, they let me go, warning us that we would be being watched. We missed our train to Paris but it gave us the opportunity to visit cheap-booze warehouses in Calais.

By the time we got to Paris, we were all really pissed and acting like the typical Brit abroad – although we are definitely *not* British! We somehow managed to find our way between the two major train stations in Paris without too much trouble and then planned to get an overnight train to Milan or Turin for connections to Genoa. This meant we had a couple of hours to spend in Paris. We found a pub in the station where we met a couple of French who had spotted our Celtic hats.

I suppose we got a bit rowdy, which led to the landlord refusing to serve us any more. The French cops were soon on the scene and certainly weren't to be messed with. We thought we were going to be nicked without even making Italy when, for the second time that day, Gordon came to the rescue. He produced a plastic card from his wallet, which I now know was little more than a membership card for the official

Scotland Travel Club, and told the gendarmes that we were the Scottish Youth Team and he was an SFA official. They had no reason to disbelieve him. We were then given an armed escort on to the train while the French lads got lifted.

The journey through France was mostly quiet, as we slept for most of it. We arrived in Turin in the early morning for our connection to Genoa. All signs of a hangover were soon forgotten when we got on the connecting train. It was packed full of Brazil fans, including the bikini-clad blondes we had seen on the television back home but had never dreamed we would be sharing a steamy train compartment with. It quickly made us forget about the gruelling 24-hour journey we had just endured.

We arrived in Genoa and made our way to the best hotel we could find. Tonto and his girlfriend had a room booked, leaving me, Frank and Gordon to slum it together in our first 4-star hotel of the trip. Frank paid using his card and I was surprised at how easy it had been. This would help us later on.

Our next priority was to get ready cash, as we had spent all our money travelling. The hotel clerk said they had a Bureau de Change and they could accept the card as we were customers. We then went to explore Genoa, which was a strange experience. The place was awash with Scotland fans. We met a couple of lads who used to run with Celtic. They hadn't booked a hotel yet, as they had a dodgy visa card, but didn't want to risk it. I asked to look at it and asked them if they'd let me try to get tickets with it. Scotland were due to play Costa Rica the next day, but the only tickets left were £50 each.

We went to the stadium where they were selling tickets. I asked for five and handed over the visa card. The cashier handed me a piece of duplicate paper telling me to sign. He then placed it along with the card into a plastic clicker machine. He ran the handle once over before handing me the tickets along with the card and receipt. I was amazed at how easy it had been to purchase £250 worth of credit without any checks. The two lads decided to come back to our hotel and book a room using Frank's card, but allowed us to use their card to buy everything else.

The next day, we went to meet the rest of the Celtic boys who were travelling from Yugoslavia. They had booked for two weeks in the north of that country in a bid to save money, but they hadn't reckoned on it being about 14 hours away by train. By midday, we had all gathered in one of the city squares and had a mob of about 20 Celtic plus an assortment of lads from other Scotland firms, most notably Aberdeen. As usual, none of them had tickets and we had to purchase more using the card. It was farcical with us taking turns to go into the ticket office.

We made our way to the stadium attracting attention from fans in the Tartan Army, mainly because of Celtic sun hats and a green and white saltire with the words

'Celtic Soccer Crew on Tour' emblazoned across it. However, most of the banter was good-humoured. I don't think the Tartan Army were surprised at seeing a group of Casuals. I think they were more surprised at seeing Celtic hats and flags at a Scotland match – the belief being that Celtic fans don't follow Scotland and only support Ireland.

We got into the stadium and made our way to the posh seats, which were amongst Costa Rican fans and FIFA dignitaries, who probably believed that they were well away from the riff-raff. The match itself was one of the biggest shocks in Scotland's history with Costa Rica beating us 1–0.

After the match, we went back to our hotel to help ourselves to the minibar, happily swigging away in the belief that all of the drink in the fridge was free. After we had consumed all the various wines and spirits, it was time to say farewell to the Celtic lads who were based in Yugoslavia, who had to catch the train back to their resort. We parted company after agreeing to meet up again in four days for the match against Sweden, which would also be played in Genoa. There was a rumour that Sweden had a mob called The Black Army and would be up for it, so it was arranged that we would meet up with all the other Scottish mobs that day.

The day after the Costa Rica fiasco, we checked out of the hotel and decided to go to the Med coastal resorts for a few days. We did, however, book a couple of nights for the Sweden game. We also asked if we could keep valuables in the hotel safe as advised by the Foreign Office. We handed over our passports and a few other valuables, receiving in return verification of the whereabouts of our passports. This proved to be a godsend on our travels. We went to the resort of Rapallo, where the Scotland team was based, and booked into a hotel overlooking a secluded cove on the shore of the Med. We used the dodgy card without any problem as Frank could prove we had bookings in Genoa and our passports were in the hotel safe.

Once settled, we decided to go to the Scotland training camp. We were met with disappointment when we learned that training was a closed-door affair following the Costa Rica result. This, however, never stopped us. We approached the camp, which was surrounded by security and gun-toting coppers. Gordon led us to the main entrance, looking all official in his blazer and tie. We were stopped at the gate – but Gordon came up trumps again. He flashed his card, shouting 'Ecosse Bambinos', a rough translation for Scottish Youth Team.

The gate swung open and we were ushered inside into the small but smart stadium. We walked around the pitch towards the team, while slagging Mo Johnston and sharing banter with the players. Andy Roxburgh, who was the manager, clocked us and went into a rage as he headed in our direction. A few other officials got to us before he did. They saw the funny side and remarked on our cheek but asked us to leave, adding that if we waited outside they would give us some mementoes.

We left by the same gate only to be mobbed by a crowd of autograph hunters. We signed bits of paper that were thrust towards us. One girl said she didn't have any paper so I took a card from my pocket and signed it for her. We then headed for the beach, which had a private path from the hotel to a small bar. We couldn't believe that here we were, sunning ourselves on a private beach when only a few days earlier we didn't even have passports.

That night, we went for a meal then on to a club using the card. We spent that much in the club that the owner insisted on joining us with an expensive bottle from his own cellar. We partied into the early hours before retiring to our hotel with the thought of a good long lie-in ahead of us.

However, we were awakened the next morning by the telephone ringing in our room. I picked it up to hear the manager saying, 'Señor, you have visitors.'

I went down to the reception to be met with mayhem. There were dozens of young Italians all wanting autographs and photos with us. I wondered how they knew that we were staying there and quickly realised when I noticed a bundle of cards at the reception desk bearing the hotel details. I remembered picking up a couple the previous day and then signing them as we left the training camp.

That night, we went on a pub crawl with Gordon leading the way. We had been in a few bars before we stumbled into a small club down a lane. When we approached the door, a couple of bouncers were discussing how much to charge us. I overheard them and chirped in 'Venti milla' which is about 20,000 lira. They looked surprised but agreed and then tried to have a conversation with me in Italian. I could count in Italian but that was about my limit. I nodded and said 'Si' or 'No' when I felt I had to. I think they were trying to explain that the club had 'extras' and was open until dawn.

We went in and were shown to a table by a scantily clad waitress. She took our orders, and returned with a tab, asking us if we had a card for security which they would keep at the till. We handed over the Visa and sat back to enjoy our drinks. Suddenly, from behind a curtain appeared a crowd of females who approached our table. They sat beside each of us feeling our legs and flashing a bit of flesh. They all said the same thing – 'You buy drink.' We thought we had struck it lucky.

Before long, the tables were full of empty champagne bottles, costing about £100 a bottle. It didn't take a genius to work out that we were in a brothel. Gordon had fallen for one of the girls, and was promising to give her a new life in England. We had our fun then decided to leave for a real club, but Gordon stayed, saying he had pulled.

We settled the bill and reluctantly left Gordon. We could see the girls laughing at us, probably due to the amount of money they'd got us to spend, but we had the last laugh knowing it was all on a dodgy credit card.

We got back to the hotel in the early hours of the morning hoping Gordon was in his bed. There was no sign of him so we booked an alarm call. We were due to go back to Genoa and would have to find Gordon first.

The search was now on for Gordon and we split up into pairs. But we didn't need to look far because on a bench about 50 yards from the hotel was your man looking a bit dishevelled, but nevertheless still smart in his blazer and tie.

We booked out of the hotel and headed to the station to get the train to Genoa. Gordon was very quiet during the journey and was reluctant to tell us what had happened after we had left. We decided to leave him alone and made our way to the agreed meeting place in Genoa. The Yugoslav lads were there before us, along with some Shirties who had just come over from Scotland. There was supposed to be an alcohol ban that day but it had no effect as they had a massive carry-out, which they had put in the fountain to keep cool.

Our crowd were trying to cause trouble all day but the locals weren't interested. There was a mob totalling about 40 comprising mostly Celtic, with about 10 Aberdeen and a few others. We let the Tartan Army march to the stadium without us. We hoped that this would give us an opportunity to have a go at Sweden. We decided to walk around to the Swedish end in the hope we would come across their mob. We could see a mob ahead of us flying Swedish flags and singing. We assumed they were all scarfers, but decided to have a look anyway. The majority were normal fans but among them it was easy to identify their lads, who saw themselves as hooligans. They were quite shocking, resembling a crowd of porn-movie rejects. They were all wearing denim jackets with patches and a leather glove on one hand. Some had a skull and crossbones patch, but honestly they were the most pathetic mob I have ever seen.

We approached them, letting them know we were up for a fight but they cowered back saying they weren't here for trouble. A couple of smacks were given out, trying to provoke a reaction, but they just ran away.

A couple of Aberdeen were mouthing, saying we were liberty-takers. I'd had enough of them and asked if they fancied their chances with Celtic. They said no and it calmed down. A few of our lads left to get a pint when an Aberdeen boy started mouthing again. We didn't give them a second chance and were soon wading into them. We had a few more than them but that's no excuse for the feeble defence they offered. We told them to stay out of our way and informed the lads from other firms that it was OK. But I think most of them slipped away fearing they could be next to taste justice Celtic-style.

We went into the match, which threw up another shock result with Scotland winning 2–1, and then went back to the hotel afterwards without any more trouble.

The following day, we had to decide where to go next, as we had a few days before going to Turin for the match against Brazil. The two lads we had met suggested going to Ibiza, where it was all happening if you were into the rave scene.

Frank and I felt it was too risky as his card was well over the limit, even with ID, and the other card was red hot. We said our farewells and headed back along the coast to Rapallo.

Gordon, who had been quiet since the night at the brothel, finally told us what had happened. He said he had to go to Turin to meet somebody to receive money from them. The story was that he'd gone to a flat with the girl and was mugged by her pimp. He was too ashamed to tell us that he had been a fool. He had arranged to meet a friend in Turin who was bringing money for him.

We had a whip-round and departed company at the train station, not thinking for one minute we would ever see him again.

We travelled to Rapallo where we stayed one night before deciding to really push the boat out. We heard about a luxury 5-star hotel in a place called San Remo and decided to brass-neck it. We booked in using Frank's card without any problems. The choice of facilities was awesome and we could choose between tennis, golf, gym and sauna; in fact, the list was endless. It was a baking-hot day so we stopped at a bar for a drink.

It was then that we noticed we were low on ready cash. We knew that we could get money back at the hotel but it was about a 15-minute trek. Frank noticed a bank and said he would get the money there. I waited outside, pacing the streets for what seemed an eternity. Eventually, Frank came out ashen-faced. He said they had phoned through to their head office for authorisation because he didn't have his passport on him. He asked for his card back but they must have been suspicious. They came back to him and said the transaction was declined and they were going to keep the card.

We hurried back to the hotel where we quickly packed our bags. It was then we realised that I hadn't upgraded my ticket. We looked in desperation for all the money we had left, which added up to about £100, but in three different currencies. We managed to jump a train to Nice without me having to pay, but it would be harder getting to Paris.

I got on to the Paris train by flashing my passport with the old ticket sticking out the top. Everything was going fine until we were awakened by gun-wielding cops in the middle of the night. I pretended I was drunk and that I must have thrown away the wrong ticket by mistake. They weren't falling for any crap and one of them held my bag out of a door. We eventually paid for a ticket using about a third of our money.

We arrived in Paris where we faced a six-hour wait, resulting in us spending more cash. I didn't have enough for a ticket all the way to London so I bought one to Boulogne and decided to try my luck. We got to the ferry port and held back until the boat was about to depart. Frank went to the departure gate first, while I pretended to be looking frantically in my bag. The clerks were telling me to hurry up. I said I couldn't find my ticket. They told me to hand over my passport and, if I didn't find my ticket, I could buy one on board the ferry. This was perfect. At least I would be on home soil when rumbled. We made our way to the bar, spending what little cash we had left.

Frank said he thought that he could hear my name being called. I ignored it as the calls became louder and more frequent. Eventually, we docked at Folkestone where I was arrested by the waiting coppers. Frank waited to see what was happening but was told to go away after about an hour. I was held for about three hours then let out with a caution. The coppers also warned me that I would be arrested again if I attempted to board a train or bus to London without a valid ticket.

It was now mid-afternoon and I was stranded in Folkestone without any money. I decided that the best option open to me was to sell Frank's new state-of-the art ghetto blaster and vast collection of tapes that had been weighing down my sports bag. I found a second-hand music shop where I secured a good price, which was enough to cover the cost of a coach ticket to London. I also had the bonus of having some money left over to enjoy a pub meal and a couple of pints while waiting for the bus to depart.

I eventually arrived home that night after what had been a truly amazing few weeks. I spent the remainder of the summer living and working in London. Uhoomagoo had come down to stay, having been released from prison. He thanked me and Frank for the compassion we had shown by not forgetting about him when we were living the high life in Italy. He told us he would cherish the postcard we had sent him. Especially the touching words we had written – 'Wish you were here'! Yet another Dirty Bastard Club classic.

CHAPTER 7

Old firm games are always special and the first one of the 1990–91 season was no exception.

Those of us living in London arranged to travel home for the first derby match to be played at Ibrox at the beginning of September. The other lads had made arrangements to stay at their parents' for a few days. I decided not to go to my dad's following all the hassle that I had caused him. I opted instead to stay with a girl who ran about with our mob. She cleared it with her mother, assuring her that I would be no trouble.

We arrived at Glasgow Central Station on the Friday evening, all making our way to the pub on the concourse before departing late that night, having agreed to meet up the next day for the match. I was met by said girl and we headed to Buchanan Bus Station to catch a bus to her mother's house. I was soon put at ease by the warm welcome I received from her mother. She told me she had made a bed up for me in the spare room. I decided to retire for the night after sharing a few nightcaps with my hosts.

I awoke on the Saturday morning to be met with an enormous cooked breakfast waiting at the table for me. I again thanked her for her hospitality and made a mental note to remember to buy her a present. I left at about 10am to go and meet the rest of the Crew for the match. I was quite disappointed by the numbers who had turned out. There were only about 30–40 of us, consisting mostly of the lads who had formed the Baby Crew.

The match being at Ibrox meant it was a nightmare to get to if you were a Celtic fan who wasn't on a supporters' bus. We decided to board a bus and head along Paisley Road, knowing it would be teeming with Rangers fans. As we neared the Kingston Bridge, we were spotted by some ICF who were sitting in a beer garden below the bridge. The bus was caught in the traffic, thus allowing for an ever-increasing horde of Huns baying for our blood to have us in target range. They began to throw missiles at the bus, breaking most of the windows in the process. Our mob were in a bit of a panic; some were trying to get off the bus, while others were holding seats at windows to prevent more stones and bottles from hitting us. Eventually, we all managed to stumble from the bus and into the middle of a melee.

We were totally outnumbered and surrounded on all sides and taking a real beating when all of a sudden a couple of Celtic boys emerged from a car wielding baseball bats. Luckily for us, the crowd we were battling consisted mostly of scarfers and not as many ICF and they backed off.

The police arrived and escorted us through the back streets to Ibrox Stadium without further incident. We met up with more Celtic boys who had made their own way to the ground. There were about 80–100 of us now and we made arrangements to meet up after the match. Those of us with tickets went into the stadium, while those without went to a local Celtic pub.

The match itself was played at the usual frantic pace, with, if I remember correctly, Celtic sealing a 2–1 victory.

We left the match and decided to head for the junction of Paisley Road and Broomloan Road where it was already kicking off. The lads who hadn't got into the game were involved in a running battle with Rangers lads and scarfers. Bottles and bricks were flying in all directions and the police were struggling to gain control. A boy in our Crew had a rucksack from which he produced a number of distress flares. He handed them out amongst those who were willing to let them off. Some of the flares were hand-held while others fired a bright-red fiery ball of flame. This gave Celtic the incentive and we began to chase Rangers along Paisley Road.

The police then intervened with the help of the mounted division. Our mob were rounded up and herded on to the motorway flyover at the top of Broomloan Road. The police then began to ask people where they lived before sending us off in twos and threes.

A whisper went around the Crew telling everyone to head for Bellahouston Park and meet up at the Palace of Art, which was at the top of Helen Street where all the supporters' buses were parked. It was now over an hour since the final whistle went and we were still miles from the city centre with an ever-decreasing mob.

When we met up again, our Crew numbered about 50–60. We were heading down Helen Street when I was approached by wee M-T who was a Babe from the East End. He said he knew where a couple of flares were hidden and asked if I wanted them. I said I would take them. He was away for about five minutes before returning with two enormous marine-issue distress flares. I took them and attempted to conceal them in my waistband.

As we neared Ibrox Stadium, we saw a luxury coach at the main entrance with a small crowd of Celtic supporters at it. We headed along Edmiston Drive towards the bus just as the victorious Celtic players emerged from Ibrox. Most of the lads began to run towards the bus. This caused a commotion as the scarfers waiting didn't know who we were because we weren't wearing colours.

A policeman must have radioed for back-up, as within minutes we were stopped by the police and told to stand with our backs against the stadium wall. They began to search everyone and must have thought that they had struck gold when they got to me. I didn't attempt to hide or deny my guilt. I was quickly handcuffed and taken to Govan Police Station and that was when my problems began. I gave my address in London and asked for my lawyer to be informed of my arrest.

I wasn't in my cell for very long before I was taken by the CID for questioning. They kept asking me if I knew about a break-in at the Royal Ordnance Factory in Bishopton and how I'd come across two of the stolen items.

I quickly realised that I was in deep shit and asked for my lawyer before answering any more questions. My lawyer appeared on the Sunday and explained the gravity of my predicament. She said I would be remanded in custody because I gave my address as London. I asked if I could use my dad's but she said that the London address provided an alibi for me to cover the night of the break-in.

The police were keen to know where I was living during my visit. I reluctantly told them about the girl's house and assumed they would call her mother to verify my stay there. I appeared in court on the Monday and was sent to Barlinnie Prison on remand.

I tried to call the girl and her mother to explain what

had happened. I dialled the number and was puzzled when I got an unattainable tone. I decided to write her a letter but got no reply. I didn't dwell on it, thinking I'd make it up to them when I got out.

A couple of weeks into the remand I received some shocking and tragic news. I had phoned one of my friends who informed me that one of the Celtic lads had been brutally murdered. I couldn't believe what I had just heard. I didn't know Gary all that well but I did know he was a game boy who had run with the Baby Crew for a few years. I also knew he was a hardworking guy who enjoyed a drink and loved going to the football, like most lads his age. I obviously wasn't there that night; therefore, I don't think I'm in a position to comment on the events. However, I do know that the tragedy affected everyone who knew Gary, no matter how well.

My court appearance was soon upon me. I went to court expecting the worst and a substantial sentence, oblivious to the chaos and legal arguments that were taking place in the chambers while I sat in the holding cells.

My lawyer came downstairs to see me just as I was preparing to go into court. She told me that the charges were being dropped, explaining that the Crown had charged me under a by-law that only applies within a football stadium or surrounding area when there is a match taking place. She had argued that, as I was arrested over an hour after the game had ended, the charge was invalid. I knew that I had ridden my luck and was very fortunate to be released.

A few of my mates had come to court, along with my father, who as usual was there for me. We went to the nearest pub to talk things over and decide if I was returning to London or staying in Glasgow. I said I would rather stay in Glasgow but realised I had very little clothes with me and wondered what had happened to the bag I had left at the girl's house.

I soon learned why she had been blanking me. Seemingly, her mother's house had been turned upside down by the police searching for flares and the like.

The early 90s signalled the demise for most mobs in Scotland. A lot of lads had settled down with families and jobs while others had succumbed to the lure of hard drugs. Most teams still had a hardcore element but Celtic struggled to pull a decent Crew – even for the big games.

One game in particular was a trip to Tynecastle in 1991. We tried in vain to muster a good-sized Crew but had to settle for around 25 boys. We decided to get the bus through to Edinburgh and get off at Haymarket Station.

We must have been spotted coming along Corstorphine Road because, before the bus had reached the train station, a good-looking mob of Hearts were steaming towards us. The 25 or so Celtic on the bus armed themselves with beer bottles and full cans of lager that were the remnants of our carry-out and charged off the bus towards the oncoming Hearts.

We were giving as well as we got, but were struggling to get the upper hand when the police intervened and separated the two mobs. The police directed us to the train station, informing us that we had to wait until the next train from Glasgow had arrived in order for them to escort us all safely to the ground along with the fans from the train.

We didn't mind this, especially as a good proportion of the Celtic fans travelling had at one point or another run with the Crew. The train duly arrived, carrying about 80–100 Celtic fans. The police escort consisted of about three vans and about 10 officers on foot. We made our way down Gorgie Road towards the stadium with the usual chanting and banter between both sets of supporters.

A few scarfers were overdoing it, resulting in the police escort being more concerned with them. This allowed our small mob to slip the escort two or three at a time and then make our way back towards the train station. We soon all met up and went looking for Hearts. We came across about 15–20 of them standing at a pub. We steamed in but it was mostly Babes with them and they ran into the pub. Our mob smashed a few windows, foolishly claiming a victory.

We headed towards Tynecastle singing the usual songs and goading the Hearts stragglers who, like us, were late for the match. As usual, most of us didn't have tickets for the game so decided to get a carry-out and sit at the swing park on Gorgie Road. During the match, small pockets of Hearts came along but were easily chased off. We waited at the swing park until the crowd came out and for the rest of our boys to team up. The mob now numbered about a healthy 50. Buoyed up by our earlier exploits and also the extra numbers, we made our way back towards the train station.

Anybody who has travelled to Hearts will know that it can be an intimidating experience for away fans. The set-up of the stadium means that home fans exit on to the same road as opposing fans, creating a potential flashpoint. However, the 50 or so of us knew exactly what to expect.

The police had formed a cordon allowing the home fans to disperse before escorting the Celtic fans back to the train station. We had no chance of slipping our escort this time, so reluctantly we walked back to Haymarket with the rest of the Celtic fans.

On the way past the pub whose windows had been smashed in, a crowd of Hearts were standing at the doors. However, they were much older than the kids that had been chased. The police numbers ensured that there would be no chance of a ruck – at least for now.

We were all herded to the station and marched right on to the platform to await the train home. The 25 of us without train tickets decided to go along with the police instructions, allowing them to leave us at the platform, believing we would be boarding the train.

We waited for about 5–10 minutes after the train had left before making our way back upstairs, knowing that the police would have dispersed. Once outside the station, we argued amongst ourselves as what to do next. Some lads suggested we go along Prince's Street to get our bus, while others wanted to go back down Gorgie Road and see if any Hearts were still about.

Against my better judgement, we decided to go to Gorgie. We walked down the middle of the road chanting, believing we were invincible. A couple of Hearts boys appeared in front of us, inviting us to chase them. Some of our lads ran towards them. This seemed to be the signal for Hearts boys who were waiting up a hill to ambush us. We soon found ourselves being attacked from all sides as more Hearts emerged from a pub behind us. We were totally outnumbered and everyone was on their toes. Somebody in our Crew shouted, 'Get in here', meaning the pub that we had previously smashed up.

I was across the road but tried to catch up with everyone else. I ran towards the door of the pub and was inches from safety when I felt my ankles being clipped. I could feel my legs go and see the pavement coming to meet me. I tried to regain my balance but was again battered to the ground with an assortment of weapons.

I don't know how long I was down or how many people were attacking me. My only thought was survival. After what seemed an age, I heard sirens and the sound of a Glasgow accent asking if I was OK. I took me a while to regain my composure and assess what injuries I had incurred. I could see a pool of blood and realised it was probably mine. A policeman was crouched over me holding a towel to a gaping wound at the back of my head.

I was then placed on a stretcher and taken to hospital in an ambulance. To my amazement, my injuries were restricted to a gash at the back of my head, a sprained shoulder and a number of superficial cuts where somebody had tried to slash me. The most frightening thing was when the doctors showed me my leather jacket and the amount of slash marks and knife wounds on it. The jacket most probably saved my life.

I was allowed to leave the hospital after being stitched and cleaned. One of the Celtic girls had accompanied me in the ambulance and was waiting for me to get out. We made our way to St Andrews Bus Station where, on our way, we met two Hibs boys. They knew about the day's events and asked me if I wanted to stay in Edinburgh with them. I told them I just wanted to get home. They said they would walk us down to the bus station to make sure we got home safely. As we entered the station, we were met by a running battle. Hibs were chasing Celtic all over the place. The Hibs boys with me shouted at their mob and, to their credit, they backed down. Seemingly, it had kicked off on Prince's Street when Celtic chased a couple of Hibs not knowing their full mob had just come off a train. We boarded our bus home without further incident.

After the Hearts match, I decided to take a break from football and from being an active member of the CSC. A lot of the lads who had been instrumental in the early exploits of the Celtic Soccer Crew had moved on, with many of them now having commitments such as careers, mortgages and families. I was one of only a few original members still active, meaning I was attracting a lot of attention from the police and was a target for other firms.

I decided to get a job and began working as a salesman at Allied Carpets. The job involved working most weekends, which helped to keep me away from the football. There wasn't much happening on the hooligan front anyway, which made it easier for me to stay away, which I managed to do for the entire 91–92 season. However, my shop was closed by Allied in May 1992, rendering me redundant.

The build-up to the 92–93 season presented me with the temptation to get involved again with the Crew. Celtic had agreed to play in a testimonial match for Tony Mowbray as part of the deal that took the ex-Middlesbrough captain from Teesside to Glasgow. The match was scheduled for 22 July 1992 at Ayresome Park as part of the pre-season programme for both sides. A few lads who like me

The worst riot ever seen in Scottish football was the 1980 Celtic v Rangers Cup Final played at Hampden Park.

YOUVE JUST BEEN DONE BY
SCOTLANDS NO 1 SOCCER THUGS

CELTIC SOCCER CREW

KICK
TO
KILL.   Tel : 999

The plan was to head through
the quiet streets and …

'We didn't see ourselves as an organised mob – just a crowd of people who were up for a battle.'

'Old Firm' rivalry reflects bitter divide of Glaswegians.

The emergence of a group of Celtic Casuals that would became the CSC: Celtic Soccer Crew.

CSC Celtic Soccer Crew, Regards.

The indomitable Celtic support: 'We are Celtic supporters, faithful through and through.'

hadn't been active for a while expressed an interest in going down to Middlesbrough.

There was the usual talk about hiring a coach, but that would cost too much due to a number of lads wanting to leave on the Friday and stop over in Whitley Bay before heading to Middlesbrough the next morning for the match. About 15 lads had the sense to book train tickets well in advance to take them from Glasgow Central to Whitley Bay, while the rest of us who were planning to go had decided to hire a minibus for the weekend of the match. As usual, though, we waited until the day that we were to travel before looking for a hire company that could let us have a minibus for the weekend at a reasonable price. This proved to be harder than first thought. The guy who had agreed to do the driving had points on his licence, meaning that most companies were turning him down. We were beginning to worry as time wore on, when somebody suggested that we should attempt to hire a transit van. We got a transit without any difficulties, but now had to solve the problems of transporting 12 people in a van that only had three seats. One of the lads said that he had a couple of old mattresses in his garage that we could put down in the back of the van. We all piled into the transit and headed to the lad's house to get the mattresses, stopping off for a carry-out on the way before we set off for Whitley Bay.

The back of the van was remarkably comfy, or so we thought anyway until we offered a hitchhiker a lift at a service station. We had headed down the M74 towards Carlisle where we planned to take the A69 across to Whitley Bay. We had pulled into the services just north of Carlisle for the traditional piss stop and pillage from the gift shops. As we were leaving the services, we noticed a hitchhiker standing in the pouring rain holding a crudely written sign on a piece of cardboard indicating that he wanted a lift to Newcastle. Somebody in the back shouted to the driver to stop and give the guy a lift. He looked pleased and relieved as he ran through the rain towards the van. His relief turned to horror when the side door slid open to reveal the nine drunken bodies laid out in the back of the transit. We were genuine about giving him a lift; one more body wouldn't have made much of a difference. But, despite our words of reassurance, the ungrateful bastard declined our offer of a lift.

We arrived in Whitley Bay at about 8pm on the Friday night. We then split into two groups. Some lads wanted to sort out their digs, while the rest of us wanted to grab a pint. We asked the driver to drop us off at a pub in the centre of town where we said we'd wait for them to come back.

We were only in the busy bar for about half an hour when one of the lads became involved in a heated argument with a couple of locals when he was at the bar. As the argument escalated, the locals were joined by about four of their mates who had been at the pool table. More words were exchanged, prompting one of our group to headbutt one of the locals. This was a signal for the rest of us to steam in. The locals backed off and were eventually chased out of the pub. The bar staff told us to finish our drinks and leave. We naturally took our time, hoping that some of the lads who had gone to find digs would be on their way to meet us. The bar staff gave us about five minutes before they threatened to call the coppers.

We reluctantly headed towards the exit. When we opened the door and got outside, we were confronted by a mob of about 30 locals, some of them armed with golf clubs. A few bottles were thrown at us as the crowd edged forward towards us. We were forced back into the pub where we headed straight for the pool table to arm ourselves with the cues. One of our lads suggested we should try to make a break for it through the fire exit at the back of the pub. We made for the fire escape, which we burst open, taking us out of the pub and on to a lane that runs down the back of the building. We didn't have a clue which way to run; for all we knew, we could have been heading right into the baying crowd.

We shouted to each other to make sure everyone knew the idea, which was to head for the train station. We sprinted down the cobbled lane, eventually finding our way to the train station. We now had to try to find the guesthouse or hotel that the lads had booked into. We headed out of the station and towards the area where most of the guesthouses were situated. After pounding up and down countless streets, we had a bit of luck when we spotted the transit van parked up outside a hotel. The rest were in the downstairs bar. We told them of the fight we'd been in and decided it would be better if we chose to stay in the hotel bar. I could say that it was because we didn't want to get nicked, but, although that did play a part in our decision, the main reason was that we didn't fancy taking on a whole town with only 12 of us.

We settled in the bar where we were joined by a group of Londoners who had been up at the races at Newcastle and Doncaster for a few days. A couple of the Londoners were sat at a table playing cards. I asked one of my mates, Big Skelly, if he fancied joining the card school with me. I told him that we could make easy money if we played as a team, as long as the others in the school didn't suspect that we were working together. The plan was for one of us to raise the stake when it came round for a second time to indicate that he was holding a good hand. The other would stay in to prevent any of the Londoners calling the hand. The trick worked so easily that it was almost embarrassing taking the money. We sat in the bar until the early hours, only giving up the game because the hotel wanted to set the table for the residents' breakfast. We must have left the card school with at least a couple of hundred pounds each.

After the cards, me and Skelly managed to get a couple of hours' sleep before it was time to leave for

Middlesbrough. We had met up with the lads who had travelled down by train who told us that they had a great night out in the pubs and clubs of Whitley Bay without a hint of trouble. We decided it would be a good idea if the majority of the 25 or so Crew got the train to Middlesbrough, with the driver and two passengers setting off a bit earlier so they would be at Middlesbrough Station to meet us.

When we arrived at Boro, we headed to the park close to the stadium where the vast bulk of Celtic fans had congregated. There wasn't much trouble before the game apart from when we left the park to go to the ground. Outside a pub were a group of Boro lads who were chanting 'No surrender to the IRA' from behind the safety of a police cordon. Some bottles were thrown, but the police had control of the situation. We made our way into the stadium where our Crew had swelled to about 60 as we were joined by lads who had travelled down that day.

The atmosphere was pretty good-natured to begin with, but, once the game had started, it turned a bit volatile with both sets of supporters taunting one another. When the teams had left the field for half-time, a group of lads from the Celtic Soccer Crew ran on to the pitch holding aloft an Irish tricolour with 'Parkhead Border' – the name of a Glasgow gang – emblazoned across it. They ran towards an area of the ground where the Boro firm were situated. This provoked the Boro boys, who responded by invading the pitch to confront the Celtic lads. Before the police had time to react, several hundred people from all corners of the stadium were now on the pitch. The lads from the Celtic Soccer Crew grouped up, and with our numbers swelled by drunken Celtic scarfers we had over 200.

The Boro firm were now on the pitch and made a pathetic attempt to charge at us. However, as with most English firms, they made a lot of noise and were waving their arms wildly in the air, but their charge stopped a few yards short of the Celtic front-line when they realised we weren't running away. When the Celtic lads charged forward, the Boro firm offered very little resistance and were easily chased from their own pitch. The police, who were slow to react, were now on the pitch in numbers. However, rather than arresting any of the Celtic mob, they seemed more content to usher us from the field of play. After the match, the Celtic fans were held in for about half an hour before being escorted to our respective modes of transport, with our crowd joining the escort back to the train station without any further trouble.

CHAPTER 8

Towards the end of 1992, my life took a much unexpected turn. I had been out of work since being paid off in May. The DSS were putting pressure on me to find a job and had suggested that I go on a government training scheme. I wasn't keen and didn't fancy working full-time hours for just an extra tenner on top of my Unemployment Benefit. The DSS made an appointment for me to see a training adviser, but I didn't expect to find any courses that would appeal to me.

As the adviser went through all of the training schemes available, one in particular caught my attention. It was a training programme based in a day centre that cared for severely disabled adults, and the adviser arranged an interview for me. I was very interested and was offered a place on the programme, which I started in November 1992.

The training was intensive and very hands-on. I took to it like a duck to water and passed my certificates in all aspects of the care work in a matter of weeks. I was only three months into my training when a full-time post came up in the day centre. I was encouraged to apply for the job and was told by my training manager that I had a fantastic chance of getting it.

I sailed through the interview and was offered the job that day. I couldn't believe it. I had gone from a £50-a-week trainee to a £15-grand-a-year full-time care officer in the space of three months. My first priority, once I had started in my new post, was to contact Celtic Park to enquire about getting tickets for the disabled section. I had been appointed to act as the key worker to five clients in the day centre. Two of them were football crazy and supported Celtic, but had never been to a match.

I managed to get tickets from the Celtic ticket office and began to escort the two lads to most home matches. This also helped me to stay away from the CSC and gave me a real chance to get my life on the right track.

I had been living at my sister's, in Bridge of Weir, a small village not far from Paisley. I was enjoying living outside Glasgow and away from all the trouble that seemed to follow me about while I was in the city. So, when the flat next door to my sister's was put up for sale, I made enquiries about obtaining a mortgage. I had no problems at the bank and secured a 100 per cent mortgage, with me moving into the flat in a matter of weeks.

The 1993–94 season was another major turning point in the history of Celtic Football Club. There was a lot of unrest amongst the support and demonstrations against the then current Board were commonplace. The fans in the disabled section felt that they needed a voice and made moves to start up their own supporters club. Leaflets were given out amongst the disabled fans, inviting them to a meeting. The two lads who I escorted to the matches had now managed to secure season tickets and were very interested in getting involved with their own supporters club. I think having their season tickets and being involved in a club made the two of them feel as if they were now accepted by the Celtic family.

I agreed to take them along to the meetings and, before I knew what was happening, I found myself being voted on to the committee and handed the post of social convener. I helped to organise a meal at Celtic Park, where we managed to get a couple of Lisbon Lions to attend. What a transformation my life had undergone. I had been a football hooligan who was despised by the club and its supporters, but was now a respected figure in the committee of the disabled supporters club.

In March 1994, Celtic Football Club also went through a major transformation, with Fergus McCann taking over as major shareholder, disposing of the old inept Board in the process. Mr McCann had big plans for the club, launching a share issue to the fans to help fund the rebuilding of Celtic Park. I was invited, along with other committee members of the disabled supporters club, to attend a meeting at Celtic Park to discuss plans for the new stadium, such as access and viewing areas for the fans who required wheelchairs.

A couple of days after the meeting, I suffered horrific burns as a result of an accident at home in which a boiling-hot chip pan fell from the cooker, spilling on to the floor and over the lower part of my legs and feet. I was rushed to hospital and treated for burns, with the worst being to my right ankle. If I hadn't been wearing trainers, I would most likely have lost my foot. I was off work for three months as a result of my injuries. However, I was still required to complete a college course that my employers had been sending me to, which would give me an HND in Social Care if I passed the exams. The college had sent me work to do at home, but I kept putting it off. I was also expected to organise a social event for the supporters club, which I attended in crutches while I was off work.

When I returned to the day centre, I was told that I faced a disciplinary hearing on allegations of gross misconduct. I didn't stand a chance, as management from the day centre had been present at the social event and had witnessed me drinking a pint of lager. I felt sick when the management told me that my contract was to be terminated with immediate effect. I had a mortgage to pay and had just found out that my girlfriend was pregnant.

I decided to rent out my house and moved back to Castlemilk to live at my dad's. It wasn't long before I was back to my old ways and running with the Celtic Soccer Crew again.

It was now April 1996; my girlfriend was heavily pregnant and was due to give birth at any time. I decided to go to a Scottish Cup match against Hibs at Ibrox. The game was a replay after the two sides had failed to find the net in the first match, which was played on Friday, 7 April, having been moved from the traditional Saturday to accommodate TV. The replay was to be played on Tuesday, 11 April at the same venue.

On the day of the replay, I was in town with a friend when we bumped into a guy we knew from my time in a children's home. He told us that his brother, who was a long-distance lorry driver, had returned from Germany with a box full of CS gas. I let him know what pub the Crew were meeting in that night and asked him to bring along a few cans of the gas to sell to boys in the Crew. The CSC had chosen to meet in a pub on the south side of Glasgow to help avoid any attention from the police.

There were about 40 of us in the pub when the guy appeared with the cans of CS gas. He quickly sold the half-dozen or so cans that he had brought with him.

The Crew left the pub and headed to Ibrox Stadium where we were disappointed to learn that the Hibs mob, the CCS, hadn't travelled to the match.

After the game, which Celtic won 3–1, a small group of us headed into town and towards Queen Street Station on the off-chance that the CCS had travelled but had decided to remain in a pub in the city centre. There wasn't any sign of them, so we retreated to Chambers, a pub at the Merchant City end of George Square.

After a good few drinks, one of our lads, Mick, wanted to attack a group of lads in the pub who weren't looking for trouble, but were just out for a quiet drink. Mick had a can of CS gas on him and was talking about spraying it at the group of lads. I persuaded him to give the gas to me, saying I would hand it back the following day when he had sobered up. I put the can into my jacket pocket and almost forgot about it.

About an hour later, I left the pub on my own to go to my girlfriend's house. As I walked across George Square, I was stopped by two coppers who asked me a few questions regarding my whereabouts that evening before they said they wanted to search me. My heart sank as they began to rifle through my pockets. The coppers quickly found the can of CS gas, not that I had tried to conceal it. I was put into handcuffs with my arms behind my back and led to a van that they had radioed for.

As they marched me towards the van, one of the coppers was pulling on the cuffs, forcing me to bend forwards as my arms went further up my back. As we reached the van, I kicked out in an attempt to get out of the hold and straighten myself up. I hadn't noticed another copper approaching as I kicked out. I couldn't have timed it better if I had meant to kick him in the balls, but I hadn't; I was genuinely trying to free myself from the policeman's hold. Nevertheless, I had booted a policeman in the balls and they weren't interested in whether I meant it or not. I was thrown into the back of the van. As I tried to get up from the metal floor, I was struck on the head with a truncheon. That was the beginning of a long and vicious attack by the coppers who laid into me with their truncheons.

I was taken to Stewart Street Police Station where I was led to the charge desk. I had a gaping wound on my head with blood spewing from it and found it difficult to stand up because of the excruciating pain that I was experiencing. I refused to give the desk sergeant any information, insisting that I receive immediate medical attention. I was searched again, with the contents of my pockets being put on the desk in front of me. This contained my wallet with bank cards and various forms of ID. The police identified me by verifying my name with a travel pass, which had my photograph on it. I was then thrown into a cell. I was really concerned and actually a bit frightened by the amount of blood that I was losing from the head wound. The last thing I wanted to do was lie down, knowing that if I lost consciousness it could be very dangerous for a head wound.

I began to bang on my door and was making as much noise as possible. At first, the other prisoners were shouting at me to be quiet. I managed to explain that I had been given a really bad beating and needed urgent hospital treatment. Soon everybody else was banging on their doors. Eventually, a policeman came to take me to hospital. I was seen at the A&E Department of Glasgow Royal Infirmary where I received 12 stitches to the head wound. I was also X-rayed and given painkillers to ease the excruciating pain I was in as a result of a couple of bruised ribs. The A&E consultant wanted to know how I had sustained my injuries. I told him that it was a result of the police beating me with their truncheons. He told me to get photographs of my injuries, adding that he would be willing to give my lawyer an account of them.

I appeared on petition at Glasgow Sheriff Court the next day charged with possession of firearms, police assault and resisting arrest. I was remanded in custody for seven days and taken to Barlinnie. On arrival at prison, I was seen by the medical officer. He was visibly shocked when I told him how I had sustained my injuries and insisted on taking photographs, saying it was the worst case of police brutality that he had ever seen.

I spent the next seven days in Barlinnie, worrying

that I would miss the birth of my first child. My girlfriend came up to see me every day before she went into hospital on the Monday. I appeared back at court on Wednesday and was surprised to get bail. My first priority was to get to the maternity hospital, hoping that the child hadn't yet been born. I was lucky and was present at the birth of my eldest son, Sean, who made his appearance at 7.30pm on Friday, 21 April.

I waited until the Monday before I went to Stewart Street Police Station to lodge a complaint against the officers. I was seen by a female officer who was a superintendent. At first, she tried to dismiss my allegations and wanted to know why I had waited nearly two weeks to make a complaint. That was easy to explain; I had been in Barlinnie before spending time with my girlfriend and our new arrival. As I relayed my version of events to the superintendent, she seemed to be taking it more seriously and told me she would be submitting my complaint to the Fiscal.

A couple of months later, I got a letter from the Fiscal's office asking me to come in and see them. This is when I sold my soul to the devil and agreed to a deal that the Fiscal was offering me. I was reminded that I faced firearms charges and, with my record, that would result in me getting at least two years in prison. The proposition was if I dropped the complaint against the officers then the Crown would look at my charges in a favourable manner and, if I pleaded guilty to the firearms charge, the other charges would be dropped.

CELTIC SOCCER CREW

The Fiscal added that the Crown would not impose a custodial sentence but would recommend that I carry out 200 hours of community service and be placed on probation for a year. I knew my hands were tied and reluctantly agreed to the deal. I had to think of my newborn son and my girlfriend and didn't want to miss the first year of Sean's life.

CHAPTER 9

Not much happened for a couple of seasons. There were one or two incidents but nothing stands out. Like a lot of other lads, I managed to secure a well-paid, respectable job and settled down with my long-term girlfriend and our first child.

With the lack of football activity, a few lads, myself included, got involved with the far-left Red Action. This involved attacks on the scum of the British National Party and other fascist organisations, which were trying to get a foothold in Scotland.

The Celtic Soccer Crew is not affiliated to any political organisation. We always welcomed people from all walks of life regardless of race, creed or colour. The founder members were quick to ditch the original name of Roman Catholic Casuals, which we soon recognised was inappropriate, given that a lot of the lads were actually Protestants. A lot of our members have, however, been involved in one capacity or another with left-wing groups and Republican flute bands, while other lads show no interest whatsoever in politics and are strictly in the CSC for football-associated reasons only.

The founder members of the CSC had all grown up during a Thatcher-dominated era, which made it virtually impossible to escape or ignore the topic of politics. Almost every family in Scotland had been directly affected by the redundancies and strikes that blighted every workplace during the 1970s and 80s. Thatcher showed her disregard for the working class by imposing her politics of dismantling the heavy industries in the north and crushing the once powerful trade unions. This culminated in the miners' strike of 1984–85 when she decided to shut down hundreds of pits and put tens of thousands of men out of work. The miners fought for their jobs and had the support of every working-class community north of Watford. The picket lines outside the collieries soon became battle zones between the miners and the hundreds of policemen who had been deployed to protect the loathsome scabs. The strike lasted for over a year. With Thatcher remaining unbowed, the miners, broken and destitute, reluctantly accepted the closures.

Thatcher had first displayed her disregard for human life back in 1981 when she allowed 10 Irish Republican prisoners to die on hunger strike. The prisoners had spent many years on the blanket protest for the right to be treated as political prisoners. Many of them had been locked up for a number of years under the Special Powers Act which allowed the courts to impose sentences on suspected IRA members without their having a trial, or in some cases even charges made against them. In desperation, the prisoners decided to begin a hunger strike. They also put forward prisoner Bobby Sands to stand as a candidate in a parliamentary by-election. The prisoners' hopes of attaining political status were raised when Bobby Sands was elected as the MP for Fermanagh, receiving over 30,000 votes of the near 100 per cent turnout. Thatcher showed that she didn't consider the opinion of the public as being important and chose to stand idly by as the 10 hunger strikers passed away.

A lot of people in the west coast of Scotland are descended from Irish stock and have a vested interest in events in Ireland. A number of Republican flute bands were formed around the time of the hunger strike in an attempt by the Irish community in Scotland to highlight the injustices that were being inflicted upon the Nationalist people in the North of Ireland. I decided to join one of the bands, the Govan Shamrock, in 1985. I had returned to live in Pollok and had also joined the left-wing Scottish Militant Youth. Surprisingly, I learned more about politics while in the band than I did from the Militant Youth. I quickly learned that the motives and beliefs of the band weren't driven by religious bigotry or exclusively concerned by events in Ireland. The band would invite representatives from various political parties to help broaden the thinking of its members. We also learned about the political history of Scotland and would play at the march that commemorated the Scottish socialist John McLean.

I continued to be actively involved in flute bands and politics after the Celtic Soccer Crew had been formed. A lot of lads shared my beliefs and we would always have a visible presence at major left-wing demonstrations and Republican parades. The CSC could easily be identified on the anti-poll tax demos both in Glasgow and in London by the banner that we marched under. Rather than being seen to support some left-wing organisation, we chose to carry our own colours, which was a large Irish tricolour with a smaller skull and crossbones in the middle with Celtic Soccer Crew emblazoned across.

Throughout the years, the Crew have been approached by various left-wing militants who have asked for us to lend some muscle at marches or functions. I think some of them thought that we were a rent-a-mob who would march under any banner if there was a promise of a ruck. These loony lefties hadn't given a moment's thought to the fact that we might be politically aware and follow our own agenda. This was apparent around 1995–96 when the

JOHN O'KANE

Anti-Nazi League (the ANL) asked our Crew to accompany them to London for a demonstration against the BNP. I wasn't there but have been told by people who were that the ANL had distanced themselves from the 50 CSC lads as soon as it kicked off, as was expected, in Welling against right-wing activists.

The ANL had arranged for three buses to leave Glasgow on the Friday, travelling overnight in order to get to London in time for the demo on the Saturday morning. The 50 lads from the CSC were all on the same bus, while the other two were filled by a mixed bag of ANL activists, the do-gooders from the Socialist Workers' Party and other social-work-type loony lefties.

On arrival in Welling, the CSC were asked to take up position at the front of the demo. As the marchers neared their proposed destination, they were stopped in their tracks by police in full riot gear lined up across the road with several hundred right-wing activists behind them on the other side of the crowd-control barriers. A stand-off developed which soon escalated into a full-scale riot. The CSC lads were in the thick of it, while the ANL and their supporters backed off to a safe distance.

No Celtic lads were arrested at the time, but, after returning home, two of our members received visits from the London Police and were arrested for their part in the riot. After a trial that lasted a couple of days, one of the lads received a substantial prison sentence, while the other, who hadn't been in any trouble before, received probation and a community service order.

Following the Welling incident, the CSC have been more careful about which political organisations we lend our support to. The one that has benefited most from our support has been Red Action. The aims of Red Action appeal to a lot of lads in the CSC who believe that the only way to stop the fascists of the BNP is by direct action, which includes intimidation and violence.

However, football was always our first priority and, when Celtic decided to play Birmingham City at St Andrew's in a pre-season friendly in August 1995, we made an effort to muster a decent crew to travel down. A crowd of us hired a minibus and piled as many bodies into it as we could. We left Glasgow early on the morning of the game, and arrived in the Digbeth area of Birmingham just in time for the pubs opening. As the morning wore on, more Celtic lads converged on the Dubliner pub, now our base. The atmosphere was mostly good-natured, with me and Malcolm getting photos taken with the local constabulary, who looked rather bemused at the antics of the Celtic fans.

There was a rumour going about the mob that indicated the Birmingham Zulu Warriors were planning to attack at 2pm. As the time approached, we made sure all our mob were outside the pub and prepared for the impending attack. Our firm numbered between 40 and 50 – which we felt was a solid mob – with the added assurance of a couple of hundred scarfers in the vicinity.

Our plan was to place as many weapons, such as beer bottles, sticks and anything else which could be used to defend ourselves, strategically outside the pub. As the time approached, we could hear a chant of 'Zulu, Zulu' gradually getting louder as the Brummies approached. We lined up across the road armed with bottles and the like, bracing ourselves for the forthcoming attack. The chant of 'Zulu, Zulu' got louder and louder until from round the corner came hundreds of Birmingham running towards us.

As with most English firms, their charge forward came to a halt about 20 yards in front of us when they realised we weren't running away. Our Crew advanced towards the Zulus with bottles raining down on them. I think we totally shocked them as they were soon on their toes and running away. There were only about 50 of us, yet here we were running one of the biggest firms in England, which must have numbered 200–300.

The police seemed to take an age before steaming into our mob wearing full riot gear. Malcolm shouted to me, 'Watch out,' as a policeman's truncheon crashed into my back, knocking me to the ground. I was manhandled into a police van that already contained Gumsy Mick. He was struggling violently with two officers and, on seeing me, he seemed to increase his efforts.

Meanwhile, a policeman was trying to get me to sit down. I refused, resulting in him striking me again with his truncheon. I was rather pissed off by now with the police brutality and decided enough was enough. As he aimed another blow, I steadied myself before lunging forward and giving him a Glasgow kiss, causing him to fall backwards out of the door of the van.

By this time, the riot police had restored order outside and I had taken my seat in the van without further incident. Strangely enough, we were taken to the cells underneath St Andrew's Stadium. Mick and I were put into a cage-like holding cell. The police tried to put some Birmingham fans in beside us but decided against it after me and Mick charged a gate after they attempted to open it.

Eventually, we heard we were to be moved to a police station to await court on the Monday. We refused to leave the cell because the police who were to escort us were in full riot gear. After a stand-off, a Scottish sergeant gave us his guarantee that we wouldn't be harmed. We were taken to the Central Police Station, where Malcolm joined us as he had been arrested in the stadium.

We appeared in court on the Monday, where Malcolm and I got bail and Mick was remanded for a week. My joy at getting bail, however, was short-lived, as I had an outstanding warrant for an old fine. I found myself on the bus with Mick and heading to Winson Green Prison to spend the next couple of days.

I was placed in a hall for convicted prisoners while Mick went into the remand wing. Even though I was due for release on the Friday, I was expected to work on the hotplate – this involved serving up food to the rest of the prison population. I was involved in a minor altercation almost immediately when one of the English cons deliberately banged into my back with a metal serving tray. I turned towards him brandishing the large metal spoon that I was using to serve up the potatoes. Another con close to me warned me that the other guy was a bit of a nutter. However, I found myself in a position in which I couldn't back down.

I had no option but to follow the con into the kitchen and confront him. He was quite taken aback, as all bullies are when faced with someone who won't back down to them. He explained it had been an accident and offered me an apology. To be honest, I was pretty relieved.

Later on that night, I went out for recreation where again I was involved in a confrontation. I had put my name down for pool and was waiting for my game. Shortly afterwards, some mouthy English con shouted over to me, 'Oi, Jock, you're on.'

I immediately went on the defensive. Having lived in London, I found the most annoying thing about the English was the ignorant way that they called every Scotsman Jock. I said, 'Who are you calling Jock, Nigel?'

He looked very confused, pointing to the list of names on the blackboard. To my embarrassment, it was then I realised he was merely calling out what I had written, which of course was my initials: JOK.

The next few days passed without incident and I was released on the Friday. When I got home, I contacted my lawyer in Glasgow who liaised with a solicitor in Birmingham. My trial was set for November and I was warned I was looking at a substantial custodial sentence.

I roped in Big Tonto and Malcolm as witnesses and we made our way back down to Birmingham for the trial. We were put up by a Birmingham Red Action activist the night before the trial. The day came to go to court where I was met by my brief. He said he had an ace up his sleeve and this lifted my hopes.

I entered the courtroom rather apprehensively, but soon my spirits lifted after the evidence of the second police officer who clearly wasn't there when the fighting took place. She had merely copied the notes of the first officer. This became apparent under cross-examination from my solicitor when he asked her how she knew my name. She replied she had been told by the first officer. My solicitor stated that if the first officer had said I was John Smith then she would have identified me as John Smith. At this point, the magistrate halted proceedings and apologised to me, awarding costs in the process, which amounted to a few hundred pounds each for me, Malcolm and Tonto. I was absolutely elated and on leaving the court we passed the seething copper who I had head-butted.

Another success for the Dirty Bastard Club.

* * *

England were chosen to host the European Championships in 1996 and, to most people's amazement,
Scotland managed to qualify and were sensationally
placed in the same group as England.

We had a couple of months to organise some sort of
national firm. Me, Malcolm and Wee Eck made trips
through to Edinburgh to meet up with some of Hibs'
top boys. The Fat Controller, as usual, had loads of
ideas and plans, which we – in hindsight, stupidly –
went along with.

The idea was for Hibs and ourselves to join up with
Dundee's Utility, Falkirk and a number of boys from
other mobs such as St Mirren and the like. We decided
against joining forces with Hearts, Rangers and
Motherwell, as they had right-wing views and have a
number of lads actively involved in the scum that is the
BNP. We felt we could not trust these people and
believed that we could pull a sizeable Crew without
them. We also dismissed joining up with Aberdeen, as
there is a long history between the ASC and Hibs.

The Fat Controller suggested we all meet up at
High Barnet Tube Station, which is to the north of
London and less likely to attract attention from the
Old Bill. This seemed to be a good idea, as he also
said he had been in touch with Leicester and other
firms from the Midlands who would be willing to
meet us there.

We returned to Glasgow and made plans to hire a
coach for our Crew. We made a lot of phone calls to

older members of the CSC and we were confident we could muster a respectable crew for the journey south.

The plan was to leave Glasgow on the Friday prior to the match, travelling overnight on the long journey south. We met in a pub on the Gallowgate and the signs were we could fill the bus. We left at about 11pm with our mob numbering about 50, with others promising to meet us down there. The drink was flowing on the bus and, with a few lads full of E, there was a real party atmosphere.

We reached the outskirts of London at about 7am and decided to stop off at the last services on the M1 for breakfast and for everyone to freshen up. There were small pockets of Scottish lads milling around the service station. I think they thought that we were an English firm when they first saw us, but soon realised that we were Celtic when they saw the condition of some of our lads. We told them about the intended meeting point and most of them agreed to follow us there. We boarded our bus and continued on the short distance to High Barnet.

The bus pulled into the car park at the tube station, which was an ideal location as it was totally secluded, and let us park in an area off the main road away from any police patrols that may have been in the area.

The Fat Controller and a couple of Hibs boys emerged from several cars that were already in the car park. They told us that the rest of their mob would be arriving shortly. We decided to make our base at the pub across from the tube station which was ideal as it was situated in the open surrounded by a large grassy area, which allowed us to sit in the sunshine to finish our carry-outs before opening time at 11am.

It wasn't long before our numbers began to swell, as each tube arriving at High Barnet contained more and more lads from the various mobs. The Fat Controller told us he had been in contact with Leicester and they would be in the area at noon. The pub was now open and a couple of top boys from each Crew decided to sit in a remote corner to discuss our plans for the day.

The camaraderie amongst the usually opposing mobs was very good-natured and it was decided to fill a glass with money with the contents going to the first boy to make an impact against the English. We then heard that a couple of Leicester were cruising about in a car checking out our firm. A couple of lads spotted them and, eager to get their hands on the cash-filled glass, attacked the car with an array of missiles, forcing the bemused occupants to hit the accelerator and speed away in a panic.

This was the signal for all the other lads to hastily exit the pub believing that the English must be close by. The combined mob must have numbered at least 300. We rushed off in the direction in which the car had sped away.

The Fat Controller was on his mobile frantically trying to find out the location of the Leicester mob. They told him they were in the vicinity but had a police escort. We wandered the surrounding streets, more in hope than anticipation, and it wasn't long before we attracted the attention of the police who escorted us back to our base.

A few lads who had attacked the car all laid claim to the pot of cash, however, to everyone's surprise, the glass had mysteriously disappeared. The landlord of the pub was reluctant to serve us, so we all retreated to the grassy area. A lot of lads were getting restless and wanted to go to Trafalgar Square, which they knew would be packed with Scottish fans and the English mobs would most likely attempt to attack it. The Fat Controller was against this idea and opted to stay in Barnet along with a group of Hibs boys.

Meanwhile, a healthy mob of us headed for the tube station to catch a train to London. At this point, the Old Bill appeared and began to split the group, allowing about 30–50 lads at a time to board the tube along with a police escort. I ended up separated from the bulk of the Celtic boys with about 10 of us teaming up with a small Crew from Dundee. We decided to get off the tube at Camden Town in an attempt to escape our police escort. This was quite easy to do as the tube was jam-packed. We exited the tube station and headed to a pub close by.

We noticed a small mob milling about outside and decided to check them out. We approached them believing it was an English firm. We soon found out that they were Cardiff City and wanted to have a pop at the English. There was an uneasy silence until I said, 'We don't give a shit who you are, we are Celtic', and began to aim some blows in their direction. They were taken by surprise as the other lads followed suit.

It wasn't long before the Old Bill could be heard in the distance, bringing an end to proceedings. We all dispersed in opposite directions, with me finding myself on a tube heading back to Barnet. This was my first experience of facing Cardiff but would certainly not be my last.

I arrived back in Barnet at about 1.30pm and set out to find the rest of the national firm. It wasn't long before I came across the Fat Controller and the others in a big pub in the town centre. They told me that the Old Bill had prevented them from travelling to Trafalgar Square by asking them to produce match tickets before being allowed to board the train.

We had to settle for watching the game in the pub while it was kicking off all over London. To make matters worse, England won 2–0 with Scotland missing a penalty to add to our misery. A couple of lads suggested smashing up the pub while others wanted to attempt to head to London again.

The police, however, had other ideas and prevented more than two or three lads leaving the pub at anyone time. Reluctantly, we decided to stay in Barnet and wait for the return of the others and their stories of the day's events.

By this time, I was totally pissed off with the Fat

Controller and decided that, if Celtic were ever going to be involved in a national firm, then it certainly wouldn't be with him at the helm. The rest of the Celtic Crew began to return telling us of all the battles that had kicked off in and around Trafalgar Square. We managed to get a couple of battles with English fans before we left but I still felt a sense of disappointment.

This was all to change about two years later. The Fat Controller had jumped ship and organised a new national firm – this time with Rangers, Hearts and Airdrie. They attempted to slip into France from Spain for the World Cup in 1998. However, unsurprisingly, they were detected by the authorities and deported home. Nevertheless, his firm now thought that they had received the notoriety that the Fat Controller craved and that the other firms would fear them.

That was not to be the case when they came to Glasgow one Saturday afternoon when Celtic were playing Spurs in a pre-season friendly at Celtic Park. We didn't have much of a mob out with only about 15 of us going to Parkhead to check out Spurs. We were disappointed, as the London team only had a small pocket of fans – mostly scarfers.

Our small crew headed back along London Road towards the city centre. As we approached Bridgeton Cross, we were approached by a Hibs boy we knew. He told us that about 40 national firm were waiting for us in a pub just beyond the cross. He advised us that it would be foolish of us to confront them, as we were heavily outnumbered.

We quickly dismissed his concerns and continued along London Road. Although our mob was small, we weren't deterred, as it was all game boys who trusted one and other.

As we approached the pub, we could see the pitiful-looking national firm lying in wait looking confident and cocksure. This seemed to have an effect on our mob and without any hesitation we charged towards them – which they obviously didn't expect. I headed for the Fat Controller and all I can say is for a big fat bastard he can move!

I honestly believe that we were on top of them when the coppers arrived, putting a stop to the battle. A couple of our boys were nicked, including Malcolm. However, we returned to our pub feeling rather pleased with our performance.

As for the Fat Controller: I think he's still running.

CHAPTER 10

Shortly after the national firm incident, the draw for the preliminary round of the UEFA Cup was made. This can often see Celtic drawn against an unheard-of team from one of the new Soviet Republics. On this occasion, Celtic was spared the hassle of travelling to one of these outposts by being drawn against Welsh minnows Inter Cabletel. The away leg was to be played at Ninian Park in Cardiff, in order for Inter Cabletel to cash in by accommodating as many fans as possible, with an estimated 10,000 Celtic fans expected to make the journey.

Those of us in the Celtic Soccer Crew knew that Cardiff's Soul Crew would be out in force to get their revenge for the liberty that was taken in London at Euro 96. We were thinking about hiring a bus or going down by train, but we hadn't decided on anything when we heard about a football special that was being run by a travel agent. But there was a snag – in order to book tickets for the train, you had to be a Celtic season-ticket holder and a lot of our Crew didn't have season tickets. This was easily rectified, though, as we simply asked people who were unable to travel to Cardiff but had season tickets to buy the train tickets for us.

On the morning of the match, we met early at Glasgow Central Station with our Crew numbering about 20. As we waited in the queue to board the train, we noticed that the police were searching through people's bags and confiscating any alcohol. However, this didn't stop us from getting our carry-out on board. The train was to leave from the platform close to the car park on the far side of the station. While all the scarfers waited patiently in the queue, a few of us slipped out of a side exit and came back into the station via the car-park entrance which took us on to the platform that the train was leaving from, with our carry-outs intact. The train itself was a typical football special that looked as if it had been on a railway siding gathering dust since the days of the bi-annual trip to Wembley for the Scotland v England Home International; all that was missing was a steam engine at the front.

We arrived in Cardiff at about 1pm where we met up with other members of the CSC who had made other travel arrangements. We made our way to the lawns outside Cardiff Castle, where the majority of the Celtic support had taken up residence. There was no sign of trouble at this time, with the Celtic fans in good voice and making the most of the late-summer sunshine.

At about 5pm, we decided to move to a pedestrianised area in the city centre that had a few bars. A couple of Wrexham lads who had travelled down and had met up with our Crew recognised two or three lads who they knew to be members of the Soul Crew. It was obvious to us that they were out scouting to see what sort of mob we had. They were getting a bit mouthy and saying things like, 'Is this all you've got? It's not going to be worth our while.'

I wanted to smack the mouthpiece there and then, but Malcolm stopped me, saying it would be better to let them walk away and then follow them to see what pub they were going to.

I took Malcolm's advice and the 30 or so of us waited to see the direction they went before setting off in pursuit, hoping that they would lead us to the Soul Crew. One of them had obviously realised what our plan was and was on his mobile presumably to warn the firm in the pub. I actually confronted the Soul Crew lad who was on his mobile. He was a black guy, about 6ft tall and built like a brick shithouse, and would have probably knocked me out, which he almost did – not with a punch, though, but with his claim that he was on the phone to his mother when I asked him who he was calling.

CELTIC SOCCER CREW

We followed one of the other guys around a corner to a pub that the Soul Crew had gathered in. They were clearly expecting us and attempted to charge out of the front door with chairs and bottles, but we stood our ground and steamed right in, forcing them back into the pub, smashing a few large windows in the process. The Soul Crew regrouped and came charging back out, some through the broken windows. A fierce battle soon developed with both firms giving as good as they got. At one point, I was on the ground with somebody about to put a broken bottle in my face. Malcolm had seen what was happening and came to my rescue, punching the guy to the floor in the process.

The police eventually intervened, ushering us into an escort with a group of Celtic scarfers. Usually, the scarfers would have nothing to do with us, but on this occasion they teamed up with the Crew. The 80 or so scarfers were from two supporters clubs who had travelled down by coach and had been in a pub together. They had been involved in a battle with some of the Soul Crew who had tried to kick it off with some of the younger scarfers who had been singing Irish rebel songs. So, along with the 30 or 40 lads in the CSC, we've got about 80 scarfers who were right up for a battle, making up a sizeable firm of over 100.

We headed towards Ninian Park, a typical British football stadium, surrounded by rows of terraced houses. The Soul Crew appeared from everywhere in small pockets attempting to attack us. We stuck together and fought as a unit, scarfers included, and a good toe-to-toe developed. During the melee, I got a sore one in the face from one of the Soul Crew who had come running behind me from one of the houses. He struck me on the side of the head then disappeared into the crowd before I had time to react. I did, however, get a good look at him as he ran off. I felt my right eye begin to swell and was struggling to see out of it as it began to close completely.

The police had again restored order and were shepherding the supporters to their respective ends of the ground. My eye was giving me cause for concern and I knew that I needed to get medical attention. My mate, Joey, took me by the arm and led me over to a steward to ask him if he could radio for a First Aider to come to my assistance. The steward opened the gate that he was stationed at and called over one of his colleagues who he instructed to take me to the First Aid station. My mate, Joey, was that concerned that he abandoned me once he realised that he had got into the ground without paying. I suppose he must have picked up some Dirty Bastard Club tips from me.

Meanwhile, I was led around the track and into the First Aid room where I was given a cold compress to hold against my swollen eye. After about 10 minutes, the steward came back into the room and asked if I was ready to go to the Celtic end of the stadium. This time, he led me round inside the perimeter fence at the front of the terrace. I was in the area where the Soul

Crew had taken up their position in the seats behind one of the goals. At this point, I noticed the wee bastard that had attacked me sitting amongst the Cardiff boys. I left the steward and made a beeline for him and began laying into him before two stewards intervened by dragging me away and promptly kicking me out of the nearest exit. I suppose I can consider myself lucky not to have been nicked or, worse still, left to the mercy of the Soul Crew, who had been slow to react but were baying for my blood as the stewards dragged me to safety.

I wandered back round to the Celtic end where I approached the steward who had let me in initially. He asked me why I had been kicked out. I made some lame excuse which he bought and opened the gate and beckoned me to go back into the ground, not realising that at no point had I shown him a valid ticket.

After the game, which I think Celtic won either 5–0 or 6–0, the police held the Celtic support in the stadium before escorting those of us who were on the train straight back to the station without incident.

The remainder of the 1997–98 season was relatively trouble-free. However, it was another momentous year for Celtic Football Club. Our bitter rivals, Rangers, had amassed nine League titles on the trot and were odds-on to make it 10, breaking the proud record that was held by Jock Stein's Celtic team of the late 1960s and 70s. To be honest, I don't think many people, including the long-suffering Celtic support, believed that Celtic had the personnel to stop Rangers from clinching the elusive tenth title. The club had appointed a new manager, Dutchman Wim Jansen, who was given the unenviable task of building a team on a shoestring budget that would be strong enough to compete with the millions that Walter Smith had at his disposal at Rangers.

One of Jansen's first signings was the dreadlocked Swede Henrik Larsson, who was brought in from Dutch side Feyenoord for the princely sum of £650,000. Larsson's Celtic career started disastrously when, minutes after coming on as a sub in his debut against Hibernian in the first game of the domestic season, he gifted the ball to the Hibs player and Celtic diehard Chic Charnley, who bulleted home a 25-yard screamer to claim a 2–1 victory for the Edinburgh side. However, after the shaky start, King Henrik's class soon proved to be the difference between the two Glasgow giants, with Celtic clinching their first Championship in 10 years, sealing the title with a Larsson-inspired 2–0 home win on the last day of the season against St Johnstone.

The scenes that followed our victory were unforgettable, not only had we won the League but also we had prevented Rangers from reaching that dreaded 10 in a row. The Celtic support for the first time in a decade could look forward to the forthcoming season with some optimism.

As part of our preparation for the 1998–99 season,

Celtic had arranged to play Leeds United in a friendly at Celtic Park. The game was to be played on a Saturday with the traditional 3pm kick-off. The Celtic Soccer Crew had made no plans whatsoever for the impending arrival of the Leeds firm. I made my way into the city centre and headed for Glasgow Cross, where a large number of Celtic pubs are located. As I approached the Tollbooth, which is an Irish bar at Glasgow Cross, I noticed groups of Leeds hooligans hanging about outside the entrance to the pub. I approached them nervously, not knowing what to expect. As I got close, one of them asked if I was Celtic and wanted to know if we had a mob out. I had a look around and could see at least 50 Leeds in the Tollbooth, with more across the road milling about the entrance to the Crystal Bells, which is another pub at the start of the Gallowgate. I told the Leeds guy that the CSC wouldn't be out in numbers that day as we hadn't expected the Service Crew to travel.

I then went into the next pub after the Tollbooth, which was called Mulveys at the time and was our local. I met about half a dozen Celtic lads who had tickets for the game and were certainly not out to cause it that day. When they left to go to the game, I went to stand at the bar in the pub, where I got talking to my dad's postman. I had just ordered another pint when I clocked a couple of Rangers lads who had opened the pub door, as one of them shouted, 'C'mon, there's Celtic, they're in here.' The doors flew open and a hail of bottles came flying into the pub causing a lot of the customers to flee into the back room in panic, many of them shielding children as young as eight who were going to the match with their fathers. I grabbed a barstool and joined the bar manager and a few of the regulars who had armed themselves with baseball bats and pool cues and were preventing the Leeds crew from storming into the pub.

The pub had a very narrow entrance, which meant, if anyone was brave enough to come in, they were faced with being battered with a pool cue or baseball bat. The Leeds Service Crew, assisted by a couple of the Rangers InterCity Firm, continued to bombard the entrance with bottles and bricks, breaking some windows and a few bottles in the gantry behind the bar. Some of the missiles were reaching far into the pub and striking some of the customers, one of whom was an elderly man in his sixties who required hospital treatment and received several stitches to a gaping wound on his forehead. We managed to hold the door until the Leeds mob eventually retreated when they heard the police sirens in the distance. The staff and regulars in the pub were absolutely livid and were busy on their mobiles, making plans for when the Leeds mob returned after the match. Word quickly spread round all the pubs in the Barrowland, which is an area awash with bars that could be classed as Celtic-minded and are frequented by some hard characters.

Slowly but surely, a steady stream of people began to

appear at the pub, not all of whom were members of the Celtic Soccer Crew, or indeed Celtic fans; they were the regulars from the other pubs who were Glasgow hardmen who didn't take kindly to a group of English hooligans trying to turn over a pub on their territory. Word had also spread through the ranks of the Celtic Soccer Crew with lads appearing at regular intervals, swelling the mob assembled in the pub to about 80. This consisted of around 40–50 Celtic Soccer Crew with the rest being made up from the pub regulars and their henchmen, who were a frightening-looking mob with most of them armed with some sort of cosh, including pick shafts, baseball bats, pool cues and even a golf club.

We all waited in anticipation behind the closed doors of the pub for the Leeds Crew to come back. We had two guys who drove taxis who were monitoring the Leeds mob and their movements, with instructions to call the pub when they got close enough. Leeds came bouncing along London Road, not thinking for one minute that a Crew of 80 lads were waiting behind the closed doors of the pub, ready to pounce at any minute. We could hear the chants of 'We are Leeds, we are Leeds' getting louder as they approached. As they neared, the doors burst open taking the cocksure Leeds firm by surprise. We piled out of the emergency exit and main doors, with many of our mob wielding clubs as we charged into the startled Leeds Service Crew. Grown men were screaming and the Leeds Crew were scampering away in all directions to escape the battering that we were dishing out to them. The Leeds lads were confused and dazed. I don't think they had ever encountered such an angry mob before.

As the fighting began to die down and the Leeds mob had scattered, we made our way back into the pub. Shortly after the battle, we noticed small groups of Leeds lads trying to sneak past the pub unnoticed in crowds of at most six at a time. One of these groups had got hold of a Celtic lad who was still outside the pub and had given him a really bad kicking, in which he sustained a serious injury to his eye that later required an operation. A group of Celtic had heard what had happened and went out of the pub to ambush the group of Leeds, who were now walking beyond Glasgow Cross and into the city centre, probably thinking that they had escaped unscathed after dishing out a kicking.

The Celtic lads had cut down a back street which brought them out on to the Trongate a few yards ahead of the Leeds boys. They steamed into them, showing no mercy. I watched from a distance because I thought they were jailbait, as the attack was in full view of the CCTV cameras that cover the city centre, with the last one just before Glasgow Cross and facing the opposite direction to where the main battle took place.

The Leeds lads were taking some beating and I felt that they had had enough. However, one of the guys with the Celtic mob, who wasn't a Crew member but one of the pub crowd, decided to give one of them a nasty reminder of his visit to Glasgow. As the Crew began to make their way back towards the pub, most of them chose to ignore a Leeds lad who was lying spread-eagled on the ground. But the pub guy had other ideas and leaned over him, before taking a step back and jumping up and bringing his two feet crashing down with brutal force on to one of the Leeds lad's outstretched legs. We could hear the sickening screams from our vantage point, which was a couple of hundred yards away. The lad's leg was clearly snapped, no surprise really when you consider the pub guy was at least 15 stone.

Most of the Crew decided to get out of the Barrowland and the adjoining area and head towards a quieter pub on the south side of the city where we could get a pint without the added fear of the police wanting to question us about the brutal assault that we had just witnessed.

CHAPTER 11

The Leeds incident in 1998 was the last significant battle that the Celtic Soccer Crew were involved in during the 1990s. The activities of most firms, not just in Scotland but throughout the British Isles, had decreased dramatically and some firms existed in name only. A lot of older lads had retired from football violence for a number of reasons. I tend to believe that most of them quite simply grew up and now found themselves with commitments, such as mortgages, careers and families. The last thing that any of them needed was the added pressure of being arrested at the football. As for me, I moved into a new house with my girlfriend and our son, Sean, in 1999. I was working as an auxiliary nurse in a nursing home. I now had my own responsibilities and was enjoying my work and family life.

Everything was going really well until one day in July 2000 when I received a telephone call at work telling me that my dad was in the Victoria Infirmary and had been given the Last Rites. I immediately left work and went to the hospital to see my dad. I knew that he didn't keep the best of health, but nothing could have prepared me for my first look at him in hospital. He was almost unrecognisable and a shadow of his usual self. He asked my sister to bring up her two kids and told me to bring Sean up with me the following evening. He said he wanted to see his grandchildren together for the final time. I couldn't get my head around it. My dad had diabetes and other treatable illnesses and was getting his blood checked on a regular basis, how could they have failed to detect the cancer that was now destroying him and was so advanced that the hospital couldn't operate?

My dad refused to give in and was still with us two weeks after he received the Last Rites. The whole family were by his bedside for most of the time as his condition worsened.

One night, my mate Malcolm and my girlfriend's brother Fred had come up to the hospital with me. My sister told me to take a break and go for a pint with my mates. We went to the Brazen Head, which is a Celtic pub in the Gorbals and not far from the Victoria Infirmary. We had a few pints before going over the road to a kebab shop to get a bite to eat before going home. While we were waiting on our food, a couple of young Neds came into the shop. They were obviously out of their faces on drink or drugs and were spoiling for a fight. We tried to ignore them but it was impossible.

An argument began, which was getting more heated by the minute, with us eventually chasing them from the shop. We went back to collect our orders. When we came out of the shop, we noticed the young Neds standing at a corner brandishing bottles. We ran at them and again they ran off. However, they kept coming back, throwing bottles and bricks at us. As we chased them again, one of the wee bastards had come from the side of me and struck me over the head with a bottle. I was knocked out cold and don't remember too much about lying on the ground. I do recall coming round with Fred and Malcolm helping me to my feet. I knew immediately that something wasn't right. Malcolm had his car in the Brazen Head's car park and said he would give me a lift home. My head was spinning and I was struggling to remain conscious. I knew that it would be foolish of me to go home and insisted that Malcolm take me to hospital.

The nearest A&E Department was at the Victoria Infirmary. I was seen immediately and taken to get an X-ray. I could see the doctors examining the X-rays and was concerned when they called for a consultant to get his opinion. I was then told that they wanted to get a CAT scan in order to determine what injuries I had suffered. I was very concerned because I knew that they don't send you for CAT scan unless they thought you had a serious head injury. To be honest, I was absolutely shitting myself.

After the CAT scan, the consultant explained to me that I had two fractures on my skull and a bit of internal bleeding that had led to blood clots threatening the frontal part of my brain. He asked me if I had banged my head recently and I remembered that I had cracked my head off a shelf at work a few weeks earlier and had felt groggy for a few days. He said that explained one of the fractures and could make the blood clots easier to treat. He told me that I would be under observation for the next 24 hours or so to see if the blood clots dispersed naturally. I was taken to a ward that was right next to the one that my dad was in.

The following day, I appeared to be a lot better and was judged well enough to be allowed to see my dad. A porter took me through to his ward in a wheelchair. That was the last time I saw Big Andy, my dad. He appeared to recognise me as I sat by his bed. He then tightened his grip on the hand I was holding, as if he was determined to get my attention, before he said in a barely audible whisper, 'Take care. Look after Sean.' He then closed his eyes as he took his last breath. I just sat there holding his hand with tears streaming down my cheeks. The alarms had been triggered on the machines that he was wired up to. This alerted the nurses, who asked a porter to escort me back to my bed while they attended to my dad.

I was only in my bed for a couple of minutes when I had an epileptic seizure. I can't remember a thing about it. I know that I was rushed in for another CAT scan. The scan showed the seizure might have been a result of the blood clot moving. I was given an injection directly into my skull which the doctors hoped would dissolve the clots. The injections seemed to do the trick and I was allowed to leave the hospital a couple of days later.

When I got out, I was angry when I learned that my brother and sister wanted me to deal with all of my dad's business, such as submitting the forms to the benefits agency and dealing with the funeral expenses and any other financial matters.

They never gave a moment's thought for my dad's new wife, Mary, who he had married in 1993, with me being his best man. Mary was a few years older than my dad and suffered from mental-health problems. She had been in and out of Leverndale Psychiatric Hospital on numerous occasions. My brother and sister suggested that I ask for Mary to be committed full-time to Leverndale. I was disgusted at how callous and selfish the two of them were being. It was a very different story back in 1996 when my mother sadly passed away. Shortly before dying, my mum had received a substantial financial settlement in connection with the hit-and-run that she had been the victim of many years earlier. My brother and, even more so, my sister were very hands-on in dealing with all the legal and financial business back then. However, to my mind, they were now afraid that they might have to pay towards my dad's funeral because they thought he wasn't insured. They said I had more experience of dealing with the DSS than they did.

Despite only being released from hospital myself, I helped to organise the funeral and made arrangements for the mourners to return to my dad's local, The Oasis in Castlemilk, for a bite to eat and some drinks. The next few weeks after the funeral were very stressful for me. I underwent tests that confirmed that I now had grand mal epilepsy, which meant that I had to give up work until such times when the epilepsy was under control. I was also handling all of my dad's business and giving his wife, Mary, the support that she needed by making sure bills were paid and helping her to fill out the forms for her benefits. I felt that I was put under a lot of pressure and was offered no support whatsoever from my brother and sister.

Eight months after my dad's death, the stress became too much for me and I snapped. There are lots of mitigating facts that give an insight into the events that led up to my going berserk and smashing up the house, assaulting my five-months pregnant girlfriend in the process. However, in my view, there is no excuse for assaulting my girlfriend and I am deeply ashamed and sorry for what happened that day in April 2001.

On the day in question, I had been in town to buy

my son, Sean, a Celtic tracksuit for his sixth birthday. I was trying to keep it a surprise from my girlfriend, so, when she called my mobile and learned that I was in a pub, she naturally assumed that I was spending all my money on drink. She also knew that I had stopped taking my medication for my epilepsy due to the side effects I was experiencing. When I eventually decided to go home, I was in a bad mood and fairly drunk. We began to argue as soon as I got in the house, which was enough for me to blow my top completely.

I don't remember very much about what happened next; I was in a blind rage and was smashing up the house. My girlfriend tried to calm me down. She later told me that I pushed her to the floor and motioned as if to aim a kick at her before she says it was as if I realised at that moment what I was doing and managed to stop myself from kicking her. Then two police officers arrived and attempted to arrest me. I again saw red and seemed to go back into a rage, resulting in me struggling violently with the two coppers, forcing them to call for back-up. More officers arrived and I was arrested and taken to Maryhill Police Station before appearing in court the next day where I pleaded guilty and got bail.

I stayed with my mates for a couple of nights before my girlfriend called me and asked me to come home. We had a good talk and were trying to understand how I could have cracked like I did. I was relieved when she told me that she had been taken to hospital for a precautionary scan which showed everything was all right with the baby.

I called my old work and told them that my epilepsy was under control and asked if I could return to my job. They agreed and I was soon back enjoying my work.

Everything was going well and we were looking forward to the birth of our second child. We had even paid for a new cot and pram. Then, one morning, as I was preparing to go to work I found my girlfriend sprawled out on the toilet floor in agony. I knew immediately that something was wrong and phoned the hospital for advice. They told us to come straight in. I called a taxi, and we dropped Sean off at his aunt's house en route to the hospital.

On arrival, we were led into a room where my girlfriend was put on to a bed and given a scan. The nurse looked worried but said nothing before leaving the room. She returned with a senior nurse and a doctor, who confirmed our worst fears when he told us he couldn't find the baby's heartbeat. He then asked to speak to me in private while the nurses prepared my girlfriend for theatre.

The doctor was magnificent and was very honest with me, which was reassuring, when he told me that he was going to perform an emergency operation on my girlfriend. He explained to me that there was nothing he could do to save the baby. I was told that my girlfriend had suffered placental abruption which is a medical condition where the placenta breaks away spontaneously. I was numb and immediately thought back to that day when I went berserk. I told the doctor that I had assaulted my girlfriend three months earlier. He assured me that placental abruption is a condition that happens instantaneously and could not be attributed to something that happened three months previously.

The doctor then explained that he would have to deliver the baby by emergency caesarean section, but reiterated that the baby would be stillborn. He stressed that his priority now was my girlfriend and that, after delivering the baby, he would be performing an emergency and risk-prone operation to remove a massive blood clot that was in her womb. Even though he told me that the chances of my girlfriend surviving the operation were no more than 50–50, there was a confidence about the way he explained things which led me to believe the operation would be a success.

I was allowed to spend a few minutes with my girlfriend before she went into theatre. She was already feeling the effects of the pre-op medication and was very drowsy. I don't know if she could understand what I was saying as I told her how much I loved her and that I would be waiting for her when she came back. They then took her into the theatre and left me sitting with her sister-in-law who had come up to the hospital. I couldn't sit about doing nothing and feeling helpless, so I told the sister-in-law that I was going for a walk. I knew that there was a chapel in the hospital and decided to go there for a while. I have never been a religious person but I found great comfort in kneeling down at the altar and praying. I don't know who I was praying to, but at least I felt I was doing something.

After a couple of hours, a nurse came to fetch me. I was in a terrible state but was reassured by the nurse that the operation had been a success. My girlfriend was brought back to the intensive care unit. She had loads of machines wired up to her and had tubes going directly into the jugular vein on her neck. I remained at her bedside all night, having declined the offer of a bed in a nearby room. The following morning, the doctor came in and removed all the tubes after confirming the operation had been a 100 per cent success.

Later that day, a nurse told us about the stillborn baby. She said he was a boy and asked us if we would like to see him. The nurse gave us the option of talking to a counsellor who had experienced the heartache of having a stillborn baby and would be able to advise us before we decided if we wanted to see him or not. After speaking to the counsellor, who was absolutely fantastic, we decided that we wanted to see the baby. This was probably the hardest thing that I have ever experienced in my life. The nurse brought the baby in and handed him to me. He was perfect and had a mop of fair hair and looked as if he was sleeping. The nurse then asked me to accompany her to an office where she explained the procedures that I would have to follow before we could bury the baby. We had to decide on a name and then register his birth and death at the Registry Office. I also had to arrange for undertakers and for my girlfriend's parents' grave to be opened to let us bury him beside his grandparents. We decided on calling the baby Liam and laid him to rest about a week later.

After the funeral, I suggested to my girlfriend that we go away somewhere for a week's holiday to help us recover from our ordeal. I booked a caravan at a holiday park on the Clyde coast. We decided to invite my girlfriend's sister-in-law and her four kids as a way of thanking her for the support she'd given us throughout the last few weeks. The sister-in-law had been at the hospital for most of the time that my girlfriend was in and was fully informed about the reasons why she had lost the baby. She also knew about the fight that we had and was informed by the doctor that the assault had no bearing whatsoever on why my girlfriend had suffered placental abruption.

The reason I wrote about this tragic period in my life is to give me the opportunity to set the record straight and to abide by the promise I made when I began writing this book, which was that I would give an honest account of events that have affected my life. I would not be being honest if I just included the things that show me in a good light.

CHAPTER 12

M y girlfriend and I eventually split in February 2002, with me moving into a flat about a mile from her house. I was at a very low point in my life and it is no surprise that I became involved with the newly resurgent Celtic Soccer Crew. There had been a lull in the activities of most firms for a couple of years. There were, however, loads of internet sites dedicated to football hooliganism. The CSC had our own site which attracted a lot of new and some past members.

With the amount of interest that the site was generating, it was decided to re-form the Celtic Soccer Crew. The first match that the new firm attended was against Hearts at Tynecastle in April 2002. The game was on a Sunday with a 2pm kick-off to accommodate live TV coverage. We arranged to get the 11.30am train from Glasgow, which would get us into

Edinburgh just before Sunday opening time for the many pubs en route from Haymarket to the stadium. We met at about 10am in one of the few bars in Glasgow that have an 8am licence. The only condition attached to getting an early drink is that the customer must purchase a bite to eat from the breakfast menu. There was a steady stream of lads arriving which took our mob to about 50 or so by the time we boarded the train.

We arrived in Edinburgh just before 12.30pm and decided to take up residence in the bar of a hotel close to the station. As more trains and supporters' buses arrived, our Crew swelled to a very respectable 80–100. We left the hotel just before 1.30pm and made our way down Gorgie Road towards Tynecastle. As we got nearer the stadium, we noticed the Hearts firm, the Capital Service Firm, coming down the road behind us. We grouped up, readying ourselves for battle, but before things had a chance to kick off we were surrounded on all sides by dozens of the local constabulary. There were mounted police, coppers on motorbikes, plain clothes and a large number of uniformed officers, backed up by a fleet of vans. The coppers backed us against a wall and began to ask what we were doing in Edinburgh. Naturally, everyone said they were going to the match. The coppers asked us to produce our match tickets. A large number of our Crew had tickets and were allowed to continue their journey to the stadium.

Meanwhile, the 30 or so of the Crew without tickets were arrested under section 14 and taken in a fleet of vans to the West End Police Station. The officer in charge then informed us that we were being held for displaying behaviour likely to cause a breach of the peace. It's the most bizarre reason that I have ever heard to justify my arrest. The scenes at the police station were chaotic, bordering on farcical. The station didn't have enough cells to accommodate the 30 or so of us, meaning there was always a couple of lads in the corridors. The police in the station weren't prepared for the sudden influx of prisoners, which meant a lot of the lads were thrown into the cells without having been searched properly.

One of the boys still had his mobile phone on him. He called his girlfriend and asked her to put credit on the phone for him. We were then able to keep in touch with somebody who was watching the game on TV. The coppers must have been scratching their heads in bemusement every time the 30 of us cheered the four goals that Celtic scored that day. After the match, we all got out in small groups of three and four without any charges being brought. Although we never got the chance to have a go at Hearts that day, it certainly wasn't a fruitless exercise. The trip to Hearts help set the foundations for a new resurgent Celtic Soccer Crew which saw us being fairly active over the next three years or so.

* * *

CELTIC SOCCER CREW

The following season 2002–03 was very eventful for Celtic and our Crew, both on and off the park. The team, under the guidance of Martin O'Neill, made it to the UEFA Cup Final, claiming some notable scalps en route, including two Premiership teams. The first English side that we faced was Blackburn Rovers in the third round of the competition. The first leg was at Celtic Park on 31 October 2002, which Celtic won 1–0, thanks to a Henrik Larsson strike. The return leg was two weeks later on 14 November. Graeme Souness, who was now the manager of Blackburn, showed that he hadn't lost any of his pompous arrogance. He was quoted as saying the first leg was boys against men, indicating that his side were, of course, the men. Those sorts of comments are the kind of thing that fires up a Celtic side and they now headed to Ewood Park with an added fire in their belly.

We decided to hire a bus for the game down south. We didn't have many names to start with, but were confident of being able to fill the 60 seats. We arranged to meet in a pub on the Gallowgate with the bus due to leave at 10am. I got to the pub at about nine o'clock and was relieved and surprised to find the place packed, with a lot of familiar older faces amongst the crowd. We decided to keep the fare at a flat £20, which was more than enough to cover the cost of hire. There was a good few quid left over after paying the driver. Rather than keep the profit, I decided to go into an off-sales and buy a massive carry-out and a carton of fags to share amongst the Crew. We hadn't told the driver that we were going to Blackburn and decided to get him to drop us off at Preston Station, telling him we were going to Blackpool for a stag do.

We got to Preston before 3pm and ditched the bus at the station, having instructed the driver to pick us up again at midnight. We met up with about 20 or so Crew members who had travelled down by train. After a few beers in the town, our mob headed to the station to catch a train through to Blackburn, and arrived there at about 6pm. Our firm continued to swell as more lads joined us, having travelled down on supporters' buses. There must have been close to 100 of us when we departed the town centre to make our way to the ground. A few Blackburn scouts were out and about but kept their distance.

As we got closer to the stadium, we noticed a mob of about 40 Blackburn lads standing outside a pub. They obviously weren't up for a battle because when they saw our mob some of them retreated into the safety of the pub, while the remainder took to their toes and ran off in the direction of the stadium. We didn't get another chance to have a go at Blackburn before the match, which was quite disappointing, given they were the home team and by all accounts were supposed to have a firm that is respected by other mobs in England.

When we reached the entrances to the stadium, we were met by scenes of pandemonium. Thousands of

Celtic fans with valid match tickets were being refused admission by the stewards and police, due to the amount of fans who had got into the stadium with fake briefs. Seemingly, the turnstiles were controlled by a computer that kept count of the amount of people entering the stadium. The turnstiles had an automatic switch to tell when the stadium reached capacity. So, even though the thousands outside had genuine tickets, they couldn't get in because as far as the computer was concerned the stadium was full to capacity. A few of our lads were seething as they had bought valid tickets. The situation outside the ground was threatening to boil over as tempers amongst the fans began to break. At one point, one of the exit gates was forced open with a couple of hundred fans charging through and into the stadium before the police regained control.

The majority of the Crew headed to a pub where we watched the game. Celtic were absolutely brilliant and recorded a comfortable 2–0 victory.

After the match, we mobbed up and began to head back towards the stadium. We noticed a group of Blackburn lads just outside the stadium. We made a charge towards them, but didn't get far before the police intervened. The Crew were scattered all over the place as we tried to avoid being nicked. I was in a group with about six other Celtic lads. We were heading towards the town centre when we noticed a group of about 20 Blackburn close to the pub that they were in before the game. One of our lads, Disco Dave, pulled a can of CS gas out of his waistband and steamed into the Blackburn boys spraying the gas. The Rovers lads backed off coughing and spluttering. As usual, the police were quickly on the scene. We tried to mingle in with the scarfers to avoid being arrested, but to my utter disgust some of the Blackburn lads could be seen talking to the police and pointing in our direction. The coppers came over and quickly identified Disco Dave before placing handcuffs on him and leading him to a van, although I think he managed to ditch the CS gas before he got nicked. I was absolutely furious with the Blackburn lads.

I can never understand how members of a recognised hooligan firm can grass on lads from a rival mob. We are all football hooligans and are there for the same thing. There are a few unwritten rules that cover the conduct of respected firms, and top of the list is never to grass on your rivals just because they turned you over. The majority of firms adhere to this rule as most hooligans are like-minded and despise firms that have a reputation for grassing.

The rest of us got to the train station without further incident. However, we noticed that a few faces were missing. As well as Disco Dave, we learned that Malcolm had been nicked along with a couple of younger boys. We arrived back home in Glasgow in the early hours of the morning. I was in bed trying to catch up on some sleep when I was awakened by a telephone call in the middle of the afternoon from Malcolm who was on the train with Disco Dave. They had appeared in court that morning and been bailed to appear at a further date.

CHAPTER 13

After disposing of Blackburn in the third round of the UEFA Cup, Celtic went on to reach the Final against Jose Mourinho's Porto in the Spanish city of Seville. We had knocked out Celta Vigo in the third round, which meant that Celtic were still involved in European competition beyond Christmas for the first time in over 20 years.

Off the park, the CSC had been involved in some headline-making incidents such as the episode with Motherwell at Central Station in January 2003. This resulted in us attracting the attentions of the Football Intelligence Unit (FIU). They even mounted a joint operation with their German counterparts for our visit to Stuttgart in February 2003.

About 30 lads from the Celtic Soccer Crew had made the trip. However, we didn't all travel together; some had flown, while others had booked on supporters' buses, all arriving at different times. I didn't decide to go until two days before the match when my mate Wullie suggested we get a train to London and travel by Eurolines coach from Victoria Bus Station. We caught the sleeper from Glasgow, and arrived in London the morning before the match where we had a few hours to kill before boarding the coach which took us all the way to Stuttgart, getting us there early on the morning of the match.

We booked into a hotel before going into the city centre to meet the rest of the lads. The majority of the 15,000 Celtic fans who had made the trip had gathered at the main square in the heart of Stuttgart. We were walking through the square to meet the lads in some pub when we met a couple of guys who no longer went with the Celtic Soccer Crew but had been very active in the early years. One of them told me that he had been approached by Greyhead, which is the name the Crew had given the top man of the FIU. He told me that Greyhead had come over to him and addressed him by his name before saying, 'I heard your friend Mr O'Kane is in town. Where are you meeting?'

My mate was really spooked by this as he hadn't been involved in any way whatsoever with the Celtic Soccer Crew since about 1989. I had been in the children's home with this lad and he was instrumental in forming the CSC. He was also there the day that we first encountered football hooliganism back in 1984 when we had a go with the Aberdeen Soccer Casuals. He had moved from Glasgow to Aberdeen to work in the oil industry in the late 1980s and was now basically a law-abiding citizen with a wife and kids.

I was very perturbed when I was told about his meeting with Greyhead. Me and Wullie hadn't booked any tickets in advance as we had only decided to travel two days before the match. The only way that the FIU could know that I was in Stuttgart was by their being alerted by my passport being scanned at border control. This demonstrates the resources that the FIU have at their disposal.

I find it difficult to justify the amount of police officers and taxpayers' money that the authorities are ploughing into the FIU. I believe the main reasons behind it are simply financial, based on the vast amount of revenue that Celtic and Rangers generate. The two Glasgow giants contribute enormously to the Scottish economy, more so if they are both involved in the money-spinning Champions League. There would be in excess of 600,000 extra visitors to Glasgow if both teams were to qualify for the group stages where they would play a minimum of three home matches each. A large number of these fans travel from outside Glasgow, with many of them needing to stay overnight in a hotel in the city. If for any reason Celtic or Rangers were banned from the competition or there was negative publicity regarding the behaviour of the fans, the city would suffer economically with less visitors spending less money. I believe this is why so much time, effort and money is being invested in the FIU. When I look back on the 20-odd years that I was involved in football hooliganism, I cannot recall any instances where a person was killed as a direct result of violence between two rival firms on a match day. I am not attempting to belittle or condone the activities of football hooligans. What I would like to do is compare football violence to the gang culture that has plagued most of the housing schemes in Glasgow for decades. There isn't a week goes by where there aren't reports of young men being seriously hurt or even killed.

Glasgow has one of the highest murder rates per head of any city in the western world. There are young kids, some of them still at primary school, who daren't leave the house at night without first arming themselves with a weapon, the preferred choice being a knife. Most of them claim that it is for their own protection and don't understand fully the consequences of carrying a blade until they find themselves actually using it and killing someone. The police and the authorities seem unable or unwilling to put a stop to the knife culture that is ruining so many young lives. Yet they have dozens of FIU officers to cover a couple of hundred football hooligans. Is it because the majority of residents in the housing schemes may be claiming benefits and are therefore not contributing as much to the city coffers as the 600,000 supporters who visit the city? If the authorities were serious about tackling the problem of gang culture, they would give the same attention to it as they do to football hooligans. Instead, in my view, they are failing a generation of hundreds of young men in Scotland.

Nothing of note happened in Stuttgart apart from Celtic progressing to the quarter-final; despite losing 3–2 on the night, we won the tie 5–4 on aggregate.

The quarter-final paired Celtic against Liverpool. Things looked grim after the first leg when we could only draw 1–1, meaning we knew we had to score at Anfield to give us any chance of progressing. Celtic turned in one of their best performances of the season, running out worthy 2–0 winners.

We then faced Portuguese side Boavista in the semi-final where again we failed to take advantage in the home leg, missing a lot of chances in a 1–1 draw. However, with Henrik Larsson in our side, we knew we still had a chance of making the Final. The second leg was played on 24 April 2003. Boavista tried to protect their advantage and played a spoiling game which looked like working in their favour until Henrik Larsson scored the only goal of the match with about 15 minutes left, sending Celtic into the Final.

I faced a bit of a dilemma; I had reconciled with my girlfriend and she was expecting a baby which was due in August. I knew that I had to put her and the baby first, especially after the tragic events surrounding the last pregnancy. I was desperate to go to Seville but also

I didn't want to rock the boat. A lot of my mates were booking flights and making arrangements to travel to the Final almost as soon as the semi-final finished. Talk of the Final and the amount of supporters expected to travel had reached fever pitch as the day of the game got closer. My girlfriend knew how much it meant to me and said she wouldn't mind if I went. However, by that time, the airlines and travel agents had raised their fares to ridiculous prices, quoting several hundred pounds for the cheapest same-day returns, which didn't include a match ticket. I made several enquiries to bus companies, train operators and Celtic supporters' buses, but found that every available seat was booked. The only option open to me was the overpriced charter flights which I wasn't prepared to pay for, not when we had a baby on the way and all the expense that comes with a new arrival.

So, having followed Celtic all of my adult life and attended loads of European away games, I missed out on the biggest game of my life, having to resort to watching it in a pub in the Gallowgate. Reports suggest that anywhere between 50,000 and 80,000 Celtic fans had travelled to Spain for the match. I know of a couple of guys who had match tickets but could only get flights to Madrid where they found it impossible to get a seat on any connecting flights, trains or buses. They eventually got there by taxi after taking a fair bit of time and several hundred Euros each to convince the bemused driver that they were serious.

The amazing Celtic fans were a credit to themselves and the club with no arrests reported amongst the estimated 80,000 fans who had actually made it to Seville and the thousands more who were in Spain but unable to get from their resorts to Seville. Unfortunately, the match didn't go as expected and, despite a world-class display from Henrik Larsson, we lost 3–2 after extra-time.

My disappointment at losing to Porto in the Final was soon forgotten on 26 August 2003 when my girlfriend gave birth to a healthy baby whom we named Kieran.

A few weeks after the birth, I went out one Saturday with a few mates to wet the baby's head. We were in McKinnon's Bar which is at Glasgow Cross. Celtic were playing Motherwell at home that day but we had no intention of going to the match, nor did we have any plans to have a go at the Saturday Service. This, however, didn't stop the FIU from coming into the pub to hassle us and disrupt the celebrations.

I had just come out of the toilet and was walking towards my table when I heard my name being called. I looked over and saw Greyhead with a couple of his colleagues. I was annoyed by their very presence and told them to fuck off. Greyhead looked surprised and shouted over in a sarcastic manner, 'I see Mr O'Kane isn't in a good mood today.'

I again told him to fuck off, adding that I was having a private celebration to wet my baby's head, telling him that the FIU had no reason to be there. Greyhead was visibly shaken but left the pub.

The landlady then came over to our table and told us that she had been told by the police not to serve us any more drink. We drank up and reluctantly left the pub.

As I got outside, I was pounced upon by a couple of FIU who had truncheons drawn. My arms were placed behind my back and I was handcuffed before being led to a small unmarked two-door hatchback. I was placed into the back of the car and joined on either side by a couple of FIU officers. Greyhead and another FIU copper took their seats in the front, meaning there were five of us in the car. Greyhead was in the front passenger seat and was very excited as he talked on his mobile to his colleagues. I heard him tell them that there were 15 Cat C Celtic hooligans who had been removed from the pub and that he had a principal in custody.

I didn't know whether to laugh or cry. You would have thought by his actions and the language that he was using that Greyhead had just smashed an international drugs cartel. The car I was in was caught up in the heavy traffic that was heading to Celtic Park for the match. This meant that our progress to London Road Police Station was slow, with the traffic only moving a few yards at a time before coming to a stop. The copper who was driving the car had turned round to speak to someone in the back as we waited for the traffic to move. He wasn't paying attention when we moved off again and failed to notice a taxi that had stopped directly in front of us, resulting in him running into the back of it. We weren't going very fast, a couple of miles an hour at the most, meaning the damage to both vehicles was minimal.

After exchanging details with the taxi driver, we continued to the police station without further incident. When I got to the charge desk, I was asked to give the usual details before the desk sergeant said I would most likely be let out once my address had been checked out. At this point, Greyhead butted in, saying that he could verify my address. He then reeled off all my details, obviously his way of letting me know that, although I have never received a home visit from the FIU, I was being watched. I was put into a cell where I remained for a few hours before being released at about 6pm.

A couple of weeks later, I was in my lawyer's office to see him about another matter. I told him about my getting arrested by the FIU and the car crashing on the way to the police station. He asked if I was wearing a seatbelt and whether I was in handcuffs. I told him all the details before he advised me to make a claim against the FIU based on the fact that I had no way of protecting myself, as my hands were cuffed behind my back and also that it is illegal to travel without wearing a seatbelt when the car is fitted with them in the back seat. I called one of those no win, no fee companies that are frequently advertised on television. I gave them an account of what happened before they confirmed that I had a solid claim.

I had almost forgotten all about the claim, as I hadn't heard anything for a few months, when I received a letter one day from the solicitor who informed me that Strathclyde Police had accepted liability and would be prepared to settle my claim out of court on the condition that I attend a medical to assess what injuries I sustained. I went to a private clinic for the assessment and waited for word from my solicitors.

A few weeks passed before I received a letter informing me that Strathclyde Police had offered to compensate me with £1,300. The solicitor advised me to turn down the offer, saying she expected a much improved second one. I didn't want to antagonise the FIU any more than I had and decided to take the offer.

A few months later, I appeared at court for the breach of the peace charge. I was totally honest when giving my evidence and made no secret of the fact that I had told Greyhead to fuck off. My defence was that at no time had he identified himself as a police officer. However, I didn't bother to call any witnesses, meaning the magistrate had no choice but to find me guilty due to there being two police officers with corroborating evidence against me. She was, however, quite sympathetic towards me and fined me a paltry £75. Greyhead was seething, and today the lads say he is no longer visible within the FIU.

CHAPTER 14

My final involvement as an active member of the Celtic Soccer Crew was a trip to Dens Park to play Dundee on 28 November 2004. The match had yet again been moved from the traditional 3pm Saturday kick-off to the Sunday to accommodate live TV coverage. The Crew had hired a coach and planned to leave Glasgow at eleven o'clock on the morning of the game. We were expecting at least 40 lads to turn up, so it was a major disappointment when I got to the meeting place and saw less than 20 people there. A lot of phone calls were being made to find out what had happened to the 20 lads who said they were definitely going. We soon heard that a crowd of them had been out on the Saturday and had ended up at a party. Some of them had gone home in the early hours but couldn't be contacted while the others who were still in the house where the party was held were in no fit state and would have been no use to the Crew anyway.

We had to decide if the 19 of us who had bothered to turn up were willing to pay extra to cover the cost of hiring the coach and also if it was worth our while travelling with such a small Crew. The 19 of us consisted of a mix of about a dozen who had run with the Crew since the 1980s and the rest who were new recruits, having been involved for only a couple of seasons. Everybody agreed to pay the extra money and we eventually left Glasgow about 30 minutes late. The bus driver was the same guy who had taken the Crew down to London for Euro 96. He was also an ex-member of the CSC, so we had no bother asking him to ignore the traffic signs that directed the football supporters' buses to the designated parking areas via a route that avoided the city centre. He agreed to take us to the train station where we planned to park the bus and walk through the town on our way to the stadium.

We arrived in Dundee just after one o'clock and found a place to park the coach at the leisure centre which was close to the train station. We made our way through the city centre hoping to encounter Dundee's Utility firm. We checked out a few busy pubs but with no joy. We passed through the city centre without any trouble and were making our way up the steep hill to Dens Park. There was no sign of the Utility, which was disappointing, given that they had built up a reputation as a firm to be reckoned with over the past couple of years. However, our journey to the stadium hadn't gone entirely unnoticed. We were walking through the notorious Hilltown area where we had seen a couple of guys coming out of a pub as we passed on the other side of the road. One of them was on his mobile and appeared to be alerting somebody to our presence. A couple of lads in our Crew wanted to confront the guys at the pub, but were told to leave it because we were approaching the stadium and hadn't attracted any police. We were also hopeful that we would run into the Utility nearer the ground.

When we got to Dens Park, we noticed a group of smartly dressed lads walking towards us, one of whom in particular seemed to be staring at me. I didn't recognise any of them and assumed that they must be Dundee lads. I approached the guy who was staring at me and struck him in the face with a punch. It was then I realised that they were Celtic fans and that the guy I had punched was once in the same Republican flute band as me. I immediately regretted punching the guy and offered my sincere apologies. We then decided to find a pub to watch the game. After a couple of knock-backs from the bars close to the stadium, we found one that we had no bother getting into. The place was filled with Dundee fans but at no time was there any animosity as we settled down with our pints to watch the game, which finished in a disappointing 2–2 draw.

After the match, we headed back towards the city centre, hoping to find a bit of action with the Utility.

As we neared the pub in the Hilltown, we could see that the same guys were standing outside, this time with a couple of their mates. They didn't appear to be football hooligans judging by how they were dressed; nevertheless, we still approached with caution. A few words were exchanged between the group and a couple of lads from our Crew. Suddenly, more locals appeared, charging out of the pub armed with bottles and glasses that they tossed at us. We ran back at them, chasing the group into the pub where they held the doors closed. I then noticed that one of my mates, Fraser, had been hit square in the face by one of the bottles. He had a nasty gash to his forehead with blood pouring from it. I looked around the rows of shops and noticed a fast-food takeaway that was one of only a few places still open. I decided to go into the takeaway and ask for napkins which I could use to stop the bleeding.

I was still attending to Fraser when I noticed that the crowd from the pub had gathered outside, this time armed with barstools as well as bottles and glasses. All of a sudden, Fraser began to sprint towards them. This was the signal for all of the Crew to steam in. We didn't have any weapons, so I grabbed a metal bin from a lamppost and ran towards the pub, using the bin to protect myself from the bottles and glasses that were being thrown at us. The mob from the pub had shit themselves, and ran back indoors after they had tossed all their chairs and bottles. A couple of our lads picked up the discarded stools and charged right through the doors and into the pub. I found it hard to get near the doors due to the amount of people fighting to get in. Not wanting to contribute nothing, I decided I would smash the pub's windows from the outside with my metal bin. I crashed the bin against the windows a couple of times before I realised they were made of Perspex.

After a couple of minutes, and satisfied that the locals wouldn't attempt to attack us again, we regrouped before heading downhill towards the city centre. We could hear the sound of the sirens becoming louder, which told us the police were on to us. We tried to evade them and were about to turn a corner when suddenly we were boxed in on all sides by police cars and vans. They held us at the corner for a few minutes before they began to pick out people from the crowd. I was the first to be put into the back of a police car. I then watched as more police vehicles arrived, which provided enough transport for every one of our Crew to be apprehended.

We were taken to Bell Street Police Station where the 19 of us were placed into a holding area. The coppers told us that they would view the CCTV footage before deciding who was to be detained and charged and who would be free to go. Inevitably, I was one of the eight who were detained along with Fraser, Jambo, Tony, Kev, PC, Mick and Squarey. We appeared at Dundee Sheriff Court the following day, alongside one of the guys from the pub who was also charged. The nine of us tendered pleas of not guilty and were relieved to get bail considering Christmas was only four weeks away. The bail did carry conditions that banned us from attending any football matches in Scotland until the pleading hearing on 9 March 2005.

A couple of weeks before the hearing, one of my mates managed to get hold of a copy of the CCTV tape. He was to return it to his solicitor the following day but not before we managed to make a duplicate. I knew as soon as I viewed the tape that I was done bang to rights and had no chance of being found not guilty.

We appeared back at court on 9 March minus Mick and Squarey who had failed to turn up. The Crown made it clear that they would be willing to accept three not guilty pleas if four out of the seven who were present tendered pleas of guilty. I was one of the four who had no option but to plead guilty, and I expected to inform the court that day. However, most of the lawyers hadn't viewed the CCTV tapes, meaning the hearing would be adjourned for three weeks.

The six of us who had appeared out of the eight Celtic members charged made the journey back to Dundee on 28 March. We were called into the dock, but only to confirm our names, before being asked to wait outside while the Fiscal and the lawyers viewed the CCTV footage together. I sat in the foyer along with my five mates who were waiting anxiously to find out if they would be one of the lucky ones to be allowed to plead not guilty. To add to their anxiety, we learned that big Gander, the Dundee boy, had been advised to plead guilty due to the appalling record he had. This meant that three of them would be walking free.

After a short time, the lawyers emerged from the courtroom and called over their respective clients. I was then told that the lucky three would be Jambo, Tony and Fraser, who probably deserved it more than most after receiving several stitches to his head wound. The judge accepted the pleas and asked for social enquiry reports, community service assessments and reports regarding our suitability for electronic tagging for me, PC, Kev and the Dundee lad, Gander. We were ordered to appear again in three weeks' time.

We decided to go for a few drinks in Dundee before catching our train home, and asked big Gander to join us along with a couple of Utility boys who had come to the court to see how we got on. We shared a few pints with the Dundee lads, which to me demonstrates the mutual respect and camaraderie that exists between the majority of football hooligans who are like-minded. We then boarded our train back down to Glasgow.

It was on the journey home that I learned more about Kev and PC, the two lads who I would be sentenced with. Kev was in his mid-twenties and had a full-time well-paid job. He had a handful of previous convictions, but nothing serious. PC, on the other hand, was only 19 and had never been convicted of a criminal offence. He was also in full-time employment. I was certain that neither of them would receive a prison sentence and I was also optimistic at my chances of receiving a non-custodial sentence based on the idea that Kev and PC wouldn't be too harshly dealt with.

I received a letter from the Social Work Department the following week and was asked to attend their office for the reports to be compiled. The social worker told me I could view the reports before going to court. I returned to the office a couple of days prior to the hearing and received a copy of the social worker's report. I was very optimistic after reading that the social worker had recommended to the court that I be dealt with by a non-custodial sentence, adding that I was suitable for electronic tagging and a place would be made available for me if I received community service.

I met up with Kev and PC for the train to Dundee on the morning of 19 April 2005. It was also Uhoomagoo's birthday that day and I had made plans to go for a drink with him that night. Kev and PC told me that their reports had recommended a fine or probation with the option of tagging being suitable if the court chose to adopt that option. The three of us were rather confident when we entered the court room at 10.30am. We were one of the first cases to be called and were joined in the dock by Gander. However, someone's lawyer wasn't present, meaning that sentencing had to be adjourned for a couple of hours. We were told by the judge to enjoy our morning in Dundee and be back in the court to be called at 12.30pm. We didn't give a second thought to the judge's comments as we sat enjoying a pint in a nearby pub.

We returned to the court on time and were quickly called back into the dock. The Dundee guy, big Gander, was first in line. The judge listened to his lawyer's speech before handing out a three-month prison sentence. There were gasps from the public gallery as no one had expected any of us to receive a prison sentence. PC, who was next in line, received one year's probation and a whopping 200 hours of community service. Next up was Kev, who only had a few minor offences to his record and had received a very favourable report. The judge took no notice of the fact that he was in full-time employment and was willing to pay a substantial fine. He imposed a three-month sentence on the visibly shocked Kev.

I was last in line and knew I would be going to prison; the only question was for how long as I had more charges than the rest. My heart sank as I heard the judge say, 'Charge 1 – three months' imprisonment, charge 2 – three months, and finally charge 3 – three months.'

I was so shell-shocked that I didn't hear him say if they were to run concurrently or consecutively. It wasn't until we got to the cells below the courtroom that I found out the sentences were to run concurrently, meaning that I had in effect received the same three months as Kev and Gander.

It was only as we sat in the cells we realised what the judge had meant by telling us to enjoy our morning; it was because he had already decided what our sentence would be without listening to our lawyers' comments or taking into account the social work reports. Gander said he thought that the judge's comments gave us grounds to appeal the sentence and said he would instruct his lawyer to lodge appeal papers at the High Court.

CHAPTER 15

The three of us were taken to Perth Prison, which is one of the oldest jails in Scotland. The hall that we were put into had been earmarked for redevelopment and was due to be closed some time before our arrival, but had remained open due to the overcrowding problem within the Scottish penal system. It was like taking a step back in time to the Dark Ages. The facilities were very basic, with no toilets or wash hand basins in the cells, meaning that the prisoners had to endure the degrading practice of slopping out.

We arrived at Perth on the Wednesday but were assured that it would only be temporary and that we would be transferred to another prison by the Friday. However, we were informed on the Thursday that, due to an administrative error, we would not be moving until the following week. This meant the three of us had to spend the weekend in the dilapidated prison, during which I suffered an epileptic seizure because I hadn't been issued with my medication to cover the extra couple of days. I had informed the screw on the Friday that I didn't have any tablets, but was told I couldn't see a doctor until the Monday. I began to feel unwell on the Saturday night and pressed the buzzer in my cell in an attempt to attract a prison officer's attention. I heard footsteps approaching about an hour after I had pressed the buzzer. I waited in anticipation for the spyhole on my door to be raised to let me know that the screw was outside. I couldn't believe what happened next. The prison officer simply flicked off my light from the switch outside my cell door and continued along the landing without checking to see if I was all right. I pressed the buzzer another couple of times before the next thing I can remember is coming to on the floor of my cell after having a fit.

The next morning, I was absolutely incensed and requested to see the governor. I was told that they never took requests at the weekend and to submit it again on the Monday. It was a waste of time as we were moving to Lowmoss on the Tuesday morning.

Lowmoss is a low-security prison which started life as an RAF base on the outskirts of Glasgow to the north of the city. The majority of prisoners are housed in billets which were designed for the RAF personnel. Each billet houses 30 cons in rows of bunk beds lined up against the walls, giving almost no privacy to the inmates. Me, Gander and Kev were placed in the same billet but only briefly, because, a day after arriving at Lowmoss, big Gander was released on bail pending an appeal he had submitted. Me and Kev had decided against appealing our sentence, as we thought that, given the circumstances, we were fortunate not to be dealt with more severely and also didn't fancy the idea of being out for a few months, only to be told the appeal had been turned down, which would see us being returned to jail to complete the sentence. We said our farewells to Gander and, although we were envious at him getting out, we knew that we would be free in seven weeks and wouldn't have the uncertainty that comes with being released on appeal.

The billet that me and Kev were in was doing my head in. There were a lot of immature young cons who behaved like a group of hyperactive delinquent teenagers. I heard that there was a new unit in the prison that was supposed to be drug-free and was designed to cater for prisoners who weren't disruptive. I put my name down for the unit and was grateful to get a move almost immediately. The new unit was ultra-modern with spacious rooms that housed two prisoners each. There was a TV in every room and the inmates were given a key to their own doors. The remainder of my sentence flew by, due mainly to the relaxed regime that I was enjoying in the unit.

The seven weeks that I spent in prison gave me the

opportunity to look at myself and think about all the mistakes that I had made and the impact that my actions had on those closest to me. I had separated from my girlfriend yet again and was involved in a battle through the courts to gain access to my two boys. If the chances of my being allowed to see the kids had been very slim before I received my prison sentence, I knew now that they were virtually nil. All I had succeeded in doing was strengthening the case against me. It had been difficult enough due to my appalling criminal record and also the assault on my girlfriend that took place in 2001. My girlfriend's sister-in-law was the driving force behind refusing me access. She had gone as far as giving a statement to the court that claimed I was responsible for my girlfriend giving birth to the stillborn baby, even though she had been present when the doctor explained everything at the hospital. She even accepted my invite for her and her four kids to join us on holiday shortly after we lost the baby.

Appalling as that lie was, I know that I only had myself to blame. The reality was I had been a football hooligan for over 20 years and had amassed over 30 convictions, the majority of which were football-related. I had also spent countless weekends in police cells and over a year in prison if I was to add up all the time spent on remand and serving sentences. There were also numerous visits to hospital which resulted in my receiving, in total, several hundred stitches. This could have been avoided if I hadn't been involved with football hooliganism.

The culture that had first attracted me to the Casual scene had also changed beyond recognition. In the 1980s, there weren't any mobile phones or computers; everything was organised on a word-of-mouth basis. Nowadays, there is a new breed of wannabe hooligan who I refer to as the Internet Casuals. The majority of them can be compared to the dressers who used to follow every football firm during the 1980s. They would turn up every week wearing the best of gear and would be very visible in the pubs before and after games. However, when it kicked off, they were never anywhere to be seen. Some of these wannabe hooligans ran with the Celtic Soccer Crew for a number of years without ever being arrested or suffering as much as a broken nail. The Internet Casuals are very similar, except they now have a tool to exaggerate their involvement in battles that they may have witnessed from a safe distance but never actually participated in.

The Internet Casuals have lots of websites that require the browser to first answer a number of questions and provide a profile before they are allowed on to the site by the moderators. They claim that these measures are necessary for the protection of the sites and to ensure that its members are genuine hooligans and not Football Intelligence Officers. I can't believe how naive these computer geeks are. They must think that they are more intelligent than the FIU, whose primary aim is to gather information on the hooligan firms, which they attain by utilising the resources and state-of-the-art technology that they have at their disposal. I posted a message on one of the sites for the sole purpose of provoking a reaction. I deliberately put the full names of the people involved and the location of the incident that I was referring to. It didn't take long for the anonymous Internet Casuals to rise to my bait. Their replies came flooding in, all written using abbreviated text and initials of the same people that I was talking about. This proved to me how thick these people are. Do they think the police are baffled and are unable to decipher their pathetic attempts at communicating with one another in code? The rhetoric used by some of the Internet Casuals would have you believe that they are major players within their respective firms. The reality is that the majority of them have never gone toe-to-toe in their lives or spent a night in a police cell. I know of one who was a big noise on the CSC website and gave the impression he was a major player within the ranks of the Celtic Soccer Crew. Strangely enough, he hasn't been seen since he got fined a couple of hundred pounds after being arrested during a disturbance against Hearts at Celtic Park a couple of years ago.

When I was released from prison in June 2005, I was no longer a member of the Celtic Soccer Crew. I wish I had taken that step before my eldest son, Sean, was born in 1995 instead of continuing to be selfish and think that I could still behave like a single man who didn't have any responsibilities. It has taken me over a year to convince my ex-girlfriend that I have changed and the days of me being a football hooligan are in the past. I am grateful to her for now allowing me regular contact with my kids. My weekends still revolve around attending football matches, although not to cause any trouble, but to watch Sean play for a well-known Scottish club's under-12s team.

I can now look forward to the future and make plans that don't carry the risk of being cancelled as a result of me being arrested at a football match. I also hope that I can play an important role in my kids' upbringing and help to guide them towards achieving their goals and steer them away from choosing the path that I took when I was a teenager. It would be easy for me to lay the blame at somebody else's door and make excuses to justify why I became a football hooligan. That would be an easy way out, but I would be living in denial with a bitterness that would prevent me from moving forward with my life. I accept full responsibility for choosing to be a football hooligan and, if I am being brutally honest, I did enjoy most of my time spent with the Celtic Soccer Crew.

That's not to say it hasn't had a detrimental effect on certain aspects of my life. I realise how close I was to losing my children, which is a very sobering thought. I believe that the excitement and high that I got from football hooliganism was an addiction that could only be satisfied by being an active member of the CSC. How wrong I was. Being a father and watching my son score a goal for his team or when the youngest one says a new word or does something for the very first time beats anything that I experienced during my 20 years with the Celtic Soccer Crew.

OTHER FIRMS

Since Aberdeen burst on to the scene in the early 1980s as Scotland's first recognised football Casuals, every major club has carried a hooligan element. At one time or another, various firms have claimed to be Scotland's number one. This is my assessment of each firm based on my own experiences over the past 20 years or so.

ABERDEEN – ABERDEEN SOCCER CASUALS (ASC)
The birth of the ASC coincided with the most successful period in the history of Aberdeen Football Club. For the first time in a generation, a club outside the Old Firm were crowned League Champions and were lifting domestic trophies on a regular basis. Under the guidance of the legendary Alex Ferguson, Aberdeen even made their mark in Europe, lifting the

Cup Winners' Cup in 1983, after beating the mighty
Real Madrid in the Final. The early 1980s also saw
Aberdeen being tagged Scotland's boomtown due to the
North Sea oil industry. These two combined meant that
not only were the team successful but also their
supporters could afford to travel in large numbers to
matches at home and in Europe. It was on a trip to
Liverpool for a European match that the foundations
for establishing a Casual firm were laid. The founder
members of the ASC are believed to have observed
Liverpool's firm and decided to adopt their Casual
fashion. It wasn't long before Aberdeen boasted a Crew
of several hundred, all distinctive in their designer
sports gear.

The newly formed ASC travelled by train to most
away grounds in Scotland where they would run
amok, only encountering sporadic resistance from
small pockets of drunken Old Firm fans and the
terrace boot boys at other clubs. The ASC had
everything very much their own way for two or three
seasons before facing any real opposition from any
other firms. The first team to have a mob to challenge
them were, oddly enough, Motherwell, who were the
second team in Scotland to have a recognised
hooligan element, known as the Saturday Service
(SS). The battles between the ASC and Motherwell's
SS in the early days are legendary. It wasn't long
before every major team in Scotland carried a
recognised hooligan following. The formation of my

own firm, the CSC, came about largely due to an encounter that my mates and I had with the ASC in 1984, as most of the Celtic lads involved that day were founder members of the CSC.

The emergence of these new firms provided the ASC with new challenges and questioned their reputation as Scotland's number-one firm. To their credit, they responded positively and held on to their crown until about 1987. Aberdeen had the experience, organisation and, most importantly, the numbers to more than match any of the newly formed firms.

However, the ASC contributed to their own downfall when they took a liberty on a Hibs lad, which left him with serious head injuries. This provoked a reaction from Hibs on Aberdeen's next visit to Edinburgh. The Capital City Service (CCS) launched an audacious attack on the ASC which saw the Aberdeen lads literally running for their lives when they faced a Hibs mob armed with a petrol bomb which they threw at the ASC as they exited Waverly Station. Forced to retreat into the relative safety of the train station, the ASC knew that their reign as Scotland's top firm was effectively over, with Hibs now regarded as top dogs.

I don't think that the ASC fully recovered from that day in Edinburgh, although they continued to travel in large numbers, especially to Glasgow where the majority of battles that have involved the CSC and Aberdeen have taken place. I would say that the ASC continued to give a good account of themselves while in Glasgow, and the battles that I have witnessed would normally end with both firms claiming victory. That all changed at the 1990 Scottish Cup Final, which I described in more detail in chapter 6, when Celtic recorded our most emphatic victory against the ASC. As for Pittodrie, it shames me to admit that the Celtic Soccer Crew have never taken a sizeable firm up north since the scrapping of the football specials in the late 1980s. We have travelled with about 30–40 lads but I wouldn't want to embarrass myself by claiming the CSC have achieved anything of note in Aberdeen in recent memory.

The ASC also deserve credit for bucking the trend for right-wing politics that is associated with a large proportion of firms in both Scotland and England. The ASC have always regarded themselves as being fiercely patriotic to all things Scottish. They also view with contempt the sectarian bigotry that is prevalent amongst a number of clubs in Scotland, often mocking and ridiculing the supporters of clubs who insist on singing their songs of hate when visiting Pittodrie.

Overall, the ASC will always be seen as the original Casual firm and the mob that every new firm wanted to emulate. Throughout the 1980s and 90s and into the new millennium, the ASC have maintained a decent firm who are respected and held in high regard by most lads who have encountered them.

JOHN O'KANE

DUNDEE UNITED/DUNDEE FC – THE UTILITY

The city of Dundee holds the distinction of being the only city to have two football stadiums situated on the same street. There is no more than a couple of hundred yards separating Dundee's Dens Park from Tannadice, the home to rivals United, just across the road. The clubs can also lay claim to the fact that they are the only two clubs to be represented by one and the same hooligan firm. Strange as it may seem, the aptly named Utility attend the matches of both teams.

The excessive prison sentences dished out to members of the Utility for their part in a battle with the Celtic Soccer Crew in Glasgow before the 2005 Scottish Cup Final sent shockwaves through every firm in Scotland and beyond. I wasn't there that day due to the prison sentence I was serving for the disturbance, ironically in Dundee. The Utility had travelled down to Glasgow by train for the Cup Final. They were heading towards Hampden Park and had barely left the city centre when they encountered about 15 members of the CSC who were also on their way to the game, having just left about 40 Celtic lads who didn't have match tickets in a nearby pub. The Utility had a mob of about 50 giving them a 3:1 advantage over the Celtic lads. However, the 15 members of the CSC reportedly stood their ground and gave a good account of themselves in a battle that lasted anything up to 10 minutes, which is extraordinarily long for a fight at the football.

When the police eventually arrived, the Celtic lads had all managed to escape by taking advantage of their knowledge of the area. The Utility lads weren't as fortunate and were quickly rounded up by the Glasgow Police. I have heard that two FIU officers had tailed the Utility, who incidentally were supporting United that day, all the way from Dundee and had even travelled on the same train. The two FIU officers helped identify the ringleaders to the Glasgow Police.

I am not sure how many Utility were arrested but I do know that they all appeared on petition at Glasgow Sheriff Court after being detained over the holiday weekend. I think five of them were refused bail and remanded in custody in Glasgow's infamous Barlinnie Prison until their trial, which took place in front of a sheriff and jury in October 2005. The Utility lads were found guilty and received sentences totalling eight years between the five of them.

I have since heard that one of the lads wasn't a member of the Utility or even from Dundee. It has been suggested that he was an ex-member of Airdrie's 'Section B' hooligans, who happened to be in a bar at the train station when the Utility lads arrived. He seemingly tagged along with them, probably more out of curiosity than malice. To compound the Airdrie guy's bad luck, it was his 40th birthday around the day of the Final and his Section B mates had organised a party, complete with stripper for that night.

The Utility have built up a reputation for themselves

over the last 10 years. However, their trip to Glasgow for the Cup Final in 2005 was one of only a handful of instances that I know of when they have travelled by train for a match against Celtic in 20 years.

The CSC used to travel up to Dundee in the 1980s and early 90s in large numbers and run amok. On one visit around 1986, a lad from our Crew was arrested for a serious assault on one of the Utility boys. A group of about 30 Celtic lads had managed to slip away from the police escort that the 200–300 Crew were in that day, on the way back to the train station following a game against United at Tannadice. The breakaway group came across the Utility firm who vastly outnumbered them and the 30 Celtic lads steamed in, chasing the Utility firm. Unfortunately, one of the Dundee lads was caught by the CSC and received a horrific head injury as a result of having a piece of concrete allegedly dropped on him. The small group of Celtic lads hurried back to the train station after the incident with the Utility. They managed to catch the waiting football special and must have felt that they were going back home without any hassle from their battle in Dundee.

The engines were running, indicating that the train was about to depart, when suddenly the engines went silent and a number of policemen began to board the train with a couple of Utility lads with them. The copper went through each carriage conducting an impromptu ID parade with the help of the Dundee

Casuals, who soon helped identify the guilty party. The Celtic lad was arrested and led off the train in handcuffs. I heard that he later received four years in prison following his trial at the High Court in Perth.

The Celtic Soccer Crew continued to travel in large numbers to Dundee until the early 1990s when the football specials were withdrawn. There was then a notable lull in the activities of most football hooligan firms throughout Scotland until the Euro Championships in England in 1996, when the main mobs in Scotland joined up to form a national firm.

The Utility had a very healthy mob down in London with them for the meeting at High Barnet. They were also amongst the couple of hundred Scottish lads who insisted on travelling to Trafalgar Square as soon as they realised that the Fat Controller's plans to stay in Barnet weren't up to much. The Utility, along with the other Scottish firms in Trafalgar Square, proved to be more than capable of dealing with the English firms that day by standing firm and repelling any attempt by the English to attack or take over the square.

Towards the end of the 1990s, most of the major firms had virtually ceased to be active. However, the Utility appeared to flourish and had established themselves as a respected firm and were certainly one to be reckoned with by the time the resurgent firms resurfaced in the new millennium.

HEARTS – CAPITAL SERVICE FIRM (CSF)

The CSF are the firm that I have had the greatest difficulty in writing an honest and objective assessment about. I contemplated leaving the pages blank under their heading and allowing readers to draw their own conclusion. However, after a lot of thought, I have decided to give the readers an insight into why, as far as the CSC are concerned, the CSF are amongst the least-respected hooligan firms in Scotland.

I have written elsewhere in this book about the events of May 1987 when I along with three others appeared in front of the High Court in Edinburgh as a direct result of false statements that over a dozen grasses from the CSF gave to the Edinburgh Police. I concede that it could be argued that the guilty parties deserved to be brought to justice for inflicting the terrible injuries that the Hearts lad sustained that day. However, when you consider that the CSF had come back to confront the 30 CSC in a pub with a firm that numbered around 100 lads after the CSC had chased them earlier when their mob only numbered about 40, it is safe to assume that when they returned with a larger firm the CSF expected an easy victory over the 30 Celtic lads in the pub. After being turned over by the CSC, a number of the Hearts lads assisted the police in identifying four well-known faces from the ranks of the CSC, who they falsely accused of being responsible for the serious assault. They didn't care that we were innocent; they were more intent on fabricating evidence to ensure that a couple of Celtic's main boys went to prison along with a girl who once went with the CSF. The despicable low-lifes that gave false statements and were prepared to lie in court under oath should take a good look at themselves in a mirror. It has to be remembered that, prior to the Hearts lad being slashed, they regarded themselves as football hooligans and had set out that day in a mob who were expecting a fight with the CSC and who were probably intent on inflicting serious injuries on the 30 Celtic lads who they outnumbered by over 3:1. When they realised that one of their lads had been badly injured, they must have thought that, by helping the police to frame four innocent people, their consciences would be clear and they would be spared the guilt that they must have felt when they chose to run from the CSC, leaving their mate at our mercy.

The CSF proved that they only stand and fight when they vastly outnumber the CSC during a visit that 25 CSC made to Tynecastle in the 1990s. The Hearts mob only began to get the better of us when they had a firm of over 100 lads. However, the CSF weren't satisfied with running the 25 Celtic lads, who were forced to seek refuge in a pub. Unfortunately for me, I was the only person from our small Crew not to make it into the safety of the pub. I was knocked to the ground where I received the expected kicking. However, the Hearts mob weren't content with kicking me to a pulp;

they wanted blood and attempted to stab and slash me a number of times. If I hadn't been wearing a thick leather jacket, my injuries would probably have been life-threatening.

The CSC decided to go to Hearts for our first outing after re-forming the Crew in 2001. We didn't get an opportunity to have a go at the CSF that day; however, the CSC did record a noteworthy victory over the CSF at Celtic Park in 2002. I couldn't make the game that day but have spoken to a number of lads who were there. The CSC had a good mob of about 50 lads, who had met in a pub in the Gorbals area before heading to Celtic Park via Glasgow Green and Dalmarnock. The CSC arrived at the back of the car park that is used by visiting supporters. They were making their way through the parked buses when someone in the Crew noticed two minibuses driving in with what appeared to be Hearts Casuals in them. One of the Crew attempted to grab the steering wheel of one of the minibuses by reaching though the driver's open window. The rest of the Crew realised that it was the Hearts mob and began to attack the minibuses with traffic cones and other missiles. Seemingly, a young Celtic lad was grabbed by a motorcycle copper who had intervened. He'd managed to get away from the copper's grip when one of the minibuses knocked him over as it skidded wildly to escape the onslaught. My sources told me that there were about 25–30 Hearts lads between the two minibuses. They were cowering on the floor to avoid the barrage of missiles and at no time attempted to get out of the minibuses to confront their attackers. As usual, the Hearts mob chose not to fight because the odds weren't in their favour.

It has also been reported that the CSF have carried out cowardly attacks on small groups of Celtic scarfers who may have unwittingly walked along Gorgie Road after a Celtic match at Tynecastle. This displays the levels to which the Hearts firm are willing to stoop in order to claim victory over Celtic.

Overall, I would say that the CSF are the mob who refuse to conform to the unwritten but accepted codes and rules that the majority of hooligan firms throughout Britain adhere to. The CSC don't rate the CSF but we do regard them as a dangerous firm due to the wide range of dirty tricks that they have used in the past.

HIBERNIAN – CAPITAL CITY SERVICE (CCS)

The CCS are regarded as the top firm in Scotland and rightly so. They have shown a consistency and lived up to their reputation over the last 20 years. That's not to say they have an unblemished record or have never been turned over on occasion.

In the 1980s, Hibs were the firm that every other mob wanted to emulate, replacing Aberdeen who had set the trend. Some of the most memorable battles that I've been involved in have been between the CSC and the CCS. I have also had the opportunity of being an outsider allowed to join the ranks of the CCS in London for an England v Scotland match at Wembley in 1988. The CSC didn't take a Crew down south so I decided to travel with a few mates who went. We got the midnight bus from Glasgow the night before the game and arrived in London about eight o'clock in the morning.

Like most Scottish fans, me and two friends headed to Trafalgar Square, which is the traditional meeting place for the Tartan Army. The square was heaving with the drunken legions that were in full party spirit. Just before midday, I became aware of a mob entering the square that I soon recognised as the CCS. The majority of them were wearing T-shirts specially made for the occasion, sporting a verse from the Declaration of Arbroath along with a union flag modified to depict the Hibs colours with a message underneath saying, 'These colours don't run!' I asked my two mates if they wanted to come with me to introduce ourselves to the Hibs firm. They declined saying they were going to do a bit of sightseeing as it was their first time in London. We made arrangements to meet after the match and said our goodbyes. I then approached some of the Hibs lads and asked if they would mind if I tagged along. A couple of boys were against me coming with them but the lads that mattered said it would be OK.

The CCS had a good firm with them numbering over 100. There was a large police presence around Trafalgar Square so the CCS decided to make their way to Euston Station hoping to run into English firms who

had travelled from outside London. We got a tube
from Charing Cross Station to Euston, where we took
the escalator that connects the tube to the rail station
bringing us out of the tube and into the concourse. We
spotted a group of lads milling about outside the main
entrance and decided to confront them. At first, I think
they thought we were an English mob and looked
happy to see us. As we got closer, they began to back
off, realising that it was a Scottish firm approaching
them. A chant of 'CCS, CCS' went up, as the Hibs boys
began to steam into the English. They made no attempt
to stand and fight, fleeing in a panic in an attempt to
escape the CCS.

Buoyed up by their first victory, even though the
opposition was weak, the firm decided to head for the
West End. We marched through the bustling streets of
Soho on the lookout for any English firms. We
spotted a group of lads milling about the doors of a
boozer and decided to check them out. They were
obviously some firm because, as we approached,
more of them appeared at the entrance. Again, the
chant of 'CCS' began to ring out, acting as a signal
for the Hibs lads to get ready for action. The firm in
the pub, who appeared to be Londoners judging by
their accents, were now trying to steam out to
confront us. Me and a couple of the Hibs lads
detached ourselves from the firm, choosing to stay on
the opposite side of the road, crossing over once. We
were beyond the pub and able to attack the English

from another direction. The five or six of us steamed in just as the main firm attacked; this had the desired effect with the English lads now clambering back into the pub and holding the doors closed. The police must have been tailing us as a result of the fracas at Euston because they appeared very quickly and in large numbers, arresting me along with five Hibs lads who had attacked the English.

We were taken to Rochester Row Police Station where the six of us were cautioned and held in custody until the match had finished. The police let us out in pairs with me being released with the Hibs lad who I refer to elsewhere in this book as the Fat Controller. We made our way back to Trafalgar Square together where we met the rest of the CCS. They then told us all about the day's action, saying it had been wild both in and outside Wembley Stadium. Then, I had to say my goodbyes and go to meet my mates for the journey home.

The CCS were renewed for being the most organised firm in Scotland. They had earned a reputation for the way they turned over firms who travelled to Edinburgh, by springing ambushes upon them. That long walk from Waverley Station to Easter Road presented the CCS with plenty of secluded places for them to lie in wait, whether it was the wooden embankment that runs the length of London Road or beneath one of the many bridges that connect Edinburgh's Prince's Street with the historic part of the city. The CCS would lure firms into a trap by appearing to have only a small number of lads and enticing the visiting firm into chasing them straight into the waiting ambush.

The CSC had been involved in some memorable battles against the CCS in the home cities of both teams. We have recorded a number of hard-fought victories as well as some crushing defeats. I am also sure that there have been times when both firms have returned from a battle where both were feeling rather pleased with the day's events without having been able to honestly claim victory.

The CCS appeared to be in some disarray towards the end of the 1990s. They had a very good firm in London for Euro 96; however, their involvement with the Scottish national firm for the World Cup in France 1998 was a major misjudgement. The Fat Controller proved that his enormous ego matched his massive waist size when he persuaded a number of Hibs lads to form an unholy alliance with lads from city rivals Hearts, sworn enemies Rangers and lads from other firms who have been known to support far-right politics and have members who are actively involved in the BNP. This really surprised me because a large proportion of CCS lads are actively involved in the Republican movement with some of them being members of the left-wing James Connolly Society. The CCS are always visible at the annual James Connolly commemoration parade, which takes place in Edinburgh every summer, even providing stewards to protect the marches from possible loyalist attacks.

As for the national firm's plan to sneak into France undetected by travelling to Salou in Spain and hiring a coach to take them, it proved a disaster. The bus was intercepted by the police at the Spain/France border where the 50 or so lads were detained before being deported back home in a blaze of publicity. Not surprising really, when you consider that the Fat Controller was at the helm and he has always craved notoriety and publicity to satisfy his ego.

Despite this blip on their good name, it is my opinion that the CCS have proved beyond doubt that they have been the top firm in Scotland in the 20 years they've been going.

MOTHERWELL – SATURDAY SERVICE (SS)

Motherwell were the first team in Scotland to have a recognised firm to challenge the ASC. The emergence of the SS surprised a lot of people. Hailing from the west of Scotland and constantly living in the shadow of the Old Firm, Motherwell Football Club, by their own admission, are little more than a provincial club who would struggle to compete against the enormous attraction of the big two. This means that, even though the town of Motherwell boasts it own SPL team, the vast majority of football fans from that area prefer to make the trip to Ibrox or Celtic Park, turning their backs on the local team. This problem isn't unique to Motherwell but is one shared by all teams in Scotland, especially those from the west coast and the central belt, which means that clubs like Motherwell struggle to attract crowds over the 7,000 mark for home matches that don't involve either Celtic or Rangers. So it is quite remarkable that the SS were able to create a firm which numbered several hundred at its peak from a relatively small fan base. One advantage that the SS did have was that most of their lads lived close to one another and grew up together. This formed a bond and trust that they carried with them into the SS. This is something that the firms from Rangers and Celtic can't boast as a lot of the lads in the CSC and ICF come from different housing schemes in Glasgow who would normally be enemies without football.

In the early days, the SS proved to be an able opponent and most firms would always encounter a good battle when travelling to Fir Park. The CSC's first major victory over Motherwell didn't occur at a football match in Scotland but strangely enough on English soil. This was during a trip to Blackpool for the traditional September bank holiday weekend in 1987, which has been described in detail in chapter 4. This victory gave the CSC a psychological edge over the SS and I can honestly say I can't recall any instances when the SS have recorded a crushing victory against us. That's not to say the SS were a pushover or haven't put up a good fight where both firms have claimed to have done the other, or that the CSC can claim to have an unblemished record against the SS.

The SS, like most firms, were relatively inactive from the mid-90s. This is due to a number of issues like the introduction of all-seater stadiums, increased police intelligence and – the scourge of every firm – CCTV surveillance cameras, which are now present on every street corner in every town and city in Scotland, making it difficult for firms to mob up and have a go at opposing firms without being recorded. This was something I found out to my cost, when I received a three-month jail sentence in Dundee, which was based totally on the evidence caught on camera. All of these reasons were coupled with the fact that a lot of older lads had settled down, with many having commitments such as careers, mortgages and young families, and were attempting to put their days of football violence behind them.

Nevertheless, there has been a notable increase in the activities of football firms throughout Scotland since the dawn of the new millennium. Motherwell's SS have played their part in this resurgence, however, it has to be said, without much success as far as meetings with the CSC have gone. Over the past couple of years, the CSC have come up against the SS on several occasions. The one incident that stands out for me is the day both Celtic and Motherwell faced different teams in the third round of the Scottish Cup in January 2003.

CELTIC SOCCER CREW

Celtic were playing St Mirren at Celtic Park, while Motherwell were away to Kilmarnock at Rugby Park. We had a good firm that day which numbered between 60 and 80. There was a rumour going about that claimed the pathetically named LSD (Love Street Division) who used to masquerade as St Mirren's firm in the 1980s and 90s were all coming out of retirement to re-form the LSD for the visit to Celtic Park. The CSC had gathered in a pub in the Merchant City, an area towards the east of the city centre that boasts a wide variety of bars and restaurants. We waited on the word to confirm that the terrifying marauding masses of the LSD had indeed attempted to put together a firm and were in Glasgow. One of the younger Internet Casuals who was in our Crew had been in contact with a St Mirren lad via the web, and he took the call from the LSD. He told us that only a handful of St Mirren had managed to evade the police who were allegedly out in force in Paisley and were preventing people without match tickets from boarding the train to Glasgow. The St Mirren lads asked if they could come to the pub to explain why only a handful had travelled.

Shortly after the phone call, a group of about six or seven young boys approached the pub, none of whom looked old enough to get served, and it was very embarrassing. A couple of young Celtic lads confronted the St Mirren boys and told them in no uncertain terms to fuck off back to Paisley.

Disappointed, although not surprised by the no show from St Mirren, the CSC decided to turn our attention to the other firms who were passing through Glasgow that day. We remained in the Merchant City until after the football had finished, before heading to Central Station, more in hope than anticipation, to see if there were any other firms about. The majority of the Crew wanted to go into Bonapartes, which is a bar situated above retail units on the far side of the station and has a seating area on the balcony that overlooks the concourse. Me and a couple of older lads decided to stay in the bar, distancing ourselves from the rest of the Crew who were attracting a lot of attention due to a couple of younger lads who couldn't hold their drink.

We had hardly touched our drinks when we became aware of a mob entering the station concourse via escalators that serve the low level. The lads on the balcony were trading insults with the mob downstairs that we could now identify from the chants of 'SS, SS'. The chanting seemed to have an effect on the Celtic boys who were on the balcony and they began to throw bottles down into the direction of the SS. The SS retaliated by goading the Celtic boys and challenging them to come downstairs. What happened next can only be described as madness, and I am thankful that I had the sense to remain in the bar in full view of the CCTV cameras. Having thrown all their glasses and bottles, the Celtic lads decided to use the tables and chairs as missiles and began tossing them over the balcony. The station was very busy with many members of the public who were now running in all directions to seek refuge.

It wasn't long before the police appeared and a number of them were charging up the stairs and into the bar but not before a majority of the Crew had made their escape by kicking open a fire exit and fleeing down the emergency route and out into Hope Street. I had remained seated in the bar along with a couple of lads and we were prevented from leaving until the police had checked the CCTV tape to establish who was responsible for the melee. Once satisfied that none of the guilty people was still in the bar, the police allowed us to leave. I left the station, exiting into Hope Street where I could see the CSC going toe-to-toe with the SS. The police arrived and restored order, arresting just one Celtic lad, Wee Tam, who was later fined £75 for a breach of the peace.

What puzzled me most that night was something the police had asked a couple of Celtic lads who they had stopped. Seemingly, the police were having trouble identifying the firms involved; this was due to Aberdeen and Rangers being involved in a battle near George Square at exactly the same time as the CSC and SS were causing havoc at Central Station. We learned later that a couple of Rangers lads got heavy sentences for their part in the battle against Aberdeen.

There have been another couple of confrontations between the SS and the CSC over the last couple of seasons. Celtic played Motherwell on the last day of the season 2004–05. Celtic were expected to win the League that day but needed to win this match, and things were going to plan with the score 1–0 to Celtic with about three minutes left. Then the unthinkable happened: Motherwell equalised before scoring a dramatic winner moments later. This handed our bitter rivals Rangers the League Championship. Unfortunately for me (or fortunately if you consider the score), I was unable to attend that day as I was in prison seeing out the final days of a three-month sentence I had received for the incident I was involved in in Dundee. However, from what the lads in the Crew have told me, I understand that a Crew of about 60 Celtic remained holed up smack bang in the middle of Motherwell town centre for a good few hours after the match. Their disappointment at losing the League was compounded by the fact that the SS were nowhere to be seen, even though they had been mouthy in the ground. For a mob not to show when they know a rival firm are sitting in their town centre can be portrayed as a victory for the visitors.

Overall, I would give the SS credit for, first, taking the lead in Scotland and establishing a firm to tackle Aberdeen and, second, for maintaining those numbers over a period of time. The SS are probably amongst the top five or six firms over the last 20 years in Scotland.

RANGERS – INTERCITY FIRM (ICF)

It would be easy for me, and probably expected by some, to write this chapter in a manner that would illustrate the bitter rivalry that exists between Celtic and Rangers. I could take cheap pot-shots at the ICF and claim the CSC are superior to them and we have never been turned over. However, that would defeat the purpose of this book which I promised would be an honest and unbiased account of my experiences as a football hooligan over the past 20 years.

Most people are aware of the sectarian problems between Celtic and Rangers but few outside the west coast of Scotland actually know anything about the history behind the religious divide that separates the Old Firm. I will attempt to give the reader a brief insight into the events that helped to create the problem.

Not only is the Old Firm derby one of the oldest in the world, it is also one of the most volatile and intense with a history of violence dating as far back as 1909, when Celtic and Rangers had drawn 1–1 after 90 minutes in the replay of the Scottish Cup Final, which they had drawn 2–2 the previous week.

The crowd remained in the stadium expecting extra-time to be played. When the players left the pitch, it became clear to the 60,000 supporters that there wasn't to be any extra-time. The angry fans invaded the pitch, not to fight one another but as a joint demonstration of their anger. They began to tear down the goalposts and demolish wooden huts that housed the turnstiles, building fires with the debris. The fans then turned on the police and attacked the firemen who had attended to extinguish the fires, one of which was raging in the grandstand. The police took several hours to restore order and both Celtic and Rangers received fines as a result of their fans' behaviour. As for the Scottish Cup, the record books show that the SFA had taken the decision to withhold the trophy after the two clubs decided that there would be no second replay.

In the early years, Celtic and Rangers, although rivals on the pitch, worked alongside one another in a number of ways to help promote the game in Scotland. The relationship between the two sets of supporters was also nothing more then friendly rivalry. The sectarian issue which has plagued the Old Firm did not become an issue until the 1920s when, following the recession and the influx of Irish immigrants, the Catholic community in Scotland found themselves being discriminated against. With so many people out of work and only a small number of jobs available, the Protestant-owned companies could pick and choose who they hired. They openly displayed a prejudice by placing notices alongside the situations vacant board. Rangers must take some blame for fuelling the sectarian problem by their blatant refusal to sign players who happened to be Roman Catholic. The Irish immigrants naturally chose to follow Celtic, while the Protestant community chose Rangers.

Towards the end of the 1960s and into the 70s, events in the North of Ireland added a new dimension to the rivalry between Celtic and Rangers. The hatred was clear for all to see following the riot that took place on the pitch at Hampden after the 1980 Scottish Cup Final. The match ended in a 1–0 victory for Celtic, which prompted some fans to invade the pitch in celebration. The Rangers fans decided to join their victorious rivals on the pitch, sparking the worst violence ever witnessed at a football match in Scotland.

As the 1980s progressed, a new breed of football fans began to appear on the terraces, replacing the skinheads and boot boys. It was around the 1984–85 season that the InterCity Firm were formed. They would have been around a few years earlier but they couldn't think of a name to call their firm. Before long, they had a mob numbering several hundred. In a lot of ways, the ICF is very similar to the CSC with a lot of their lads coming from various housing schemes in Glasgow. This meant that there were groups of Celtic lads who maybe numbered about 30 all living in the same scheme who would fight with a group of ICF who had the same amount living in a nearby scheme. For instance, there was a large contingent of Rangers from Penilee who would regularly fight with the lads from Pollok who were predominantly Celtic Casuals.

However, match day was always the big one. In the early days, both the ICF and CSC could attract firms of several hundred and, if I am being honest, the battles between the two have seen both firms record victories, as well as a few stalemates and the occasional overwhelming victory.

The thing that separates the ICF from other firms, apart from maybe Hearts, is their scarfers. On numerous occasions, when the CSC have been involved in a battle with the ICF, the Rangers scarfers would help swell the numbers that we faced. In the 1980s, the majority of Casuals in Scotland were still teenagers or in their early twenties. The Rangers scarfers who chose to back up the ICF were more often than not grown men who were old enough to be our fathers. This, however, didn't deter the CSC.

The battles against the ICF were often more vicious than we had against other firms, due to a number of people who were prepared to carry and use knives at the football. These cowards usually tag along with their mates to the big games; they aren't football hooligans but often some Ned who lives in the same housing scheme as the Casuals. It's not just Rangers who have these blade merchants, and there have been times when the CSC have found ourselves attracting these undesirables. This means that, when you are charging in, to go toe-to-toe, you are aware of the possibilities that there might be blades involved, as I have learned to my cost a number of times.

But, unlike some members of the ICF, I regard any injuries that I receive as an occupational hazard and I am well aware of the risks I am taking when I choose to get involved in a battle with another firm. The exception, though, is when the injuries have been the result of a firm taking a liberty, for instance when I walked into a pub one day around 1999–2000, with a colleague from work who is a Geordie guy and not remotely interested in football hooliganism or any type of violence for that matter. My mate went to the toilet while I made my way to the bar. I became aware of a hostile group of men approaching me from all directions. I quickly realised that I had stumbled into a pub that happened to be teeming with about 30 members of the ICF. One of them did try to signal in an effort to warn me about the danger I was in. Before I had time to react, I was surrounded and found myself backing off towards the door. One of the ICF then asked me if I wanted a square go with him. I pointed out that there were 30 of them and that didn't seem like a square go to me. Ten or 20 and I may have considered his offer. Satire apart, I knew I was up shit creek.

As I was trying to talk my way out of the situation, a guy from within the group lunged forward and struck me over the head with a bottle. I was expecting a punch or a kick but for a crowd of 30 to resort to using weapons on one defenceless rival really leaves a bad taste in the mouth.

There was also an incident after the Old Firm game in January 2003. It was the first time in years that both firms had a healthy mob and there wasn't any police in the vicinity. Arrangements were made for the ICF and the CSC to meet in the Merchant City. We made our way from our base at Glasgow Cross with about 50–60 good lads. As we neared the meeting point, we noticed a few large bins outside of a pub which were full to the brim with empty bottles. A few of the Crew began to arm themselves with the contents of the bin. However, they were told by other Crew members, myself included, to drop the bottles, as we'd agreed there would be no weapons and felt confident that we could do the ICF with the mob we had.

How naive and stupid we were, for, when we turned the corner and into the street where we knew the ICF would be, we were met by a hail of missiles that was reminiscent of a scene from the movie *Braveheart* when the English ordered in the archers. To our own credit, the Crew charged towards the ICF and tried to put up a fight; however, the ICF were positioned next to a building site, giving them a plentiful supply of granite cobblestones which they relentlessly continued to launch in our direction.

The CSC had no option but to back off to escape the constant barrage. We tried to regroup but by then the police sirens could be heard in the distance. A few of our lads had also been hurt as a result of the bricks being thrown at us. I had been struck on the side by one of the missiles leaving me with bruised ribs, but that was nothing compared to another member of our Crew who had an injury to his head which required urgent medical attention. I later heard that he needed an operation and had a metal plate inserted. The ICF were no doubt pleased with their victory, whereas our lot were left to lick our wounds feeling annoyed at our decision to go into the fight without the bottles.

Overall, I would say that the ICF would have earned a lot more respect from other firms if they had refrained from using weapons and taking liberties. They have the makings of a good firm and also the numbers, and they are probably the firm who have caused the CSC the most problems throughout the last 20 years.

THE OTHER MOBS

There are a number of firms in Scotland who have been active for most of the 20 years that I was involved with the CSC. However, my personal experiences involving the firms who follow the so-called smaller clubs in Scotland has been very limited. I will give a brief account of the 'smaller firms' based mostly on reputations and my limited contact with them.

Airdrie United – Section B

The Section B were an infamous group of terrace boot boys and skinheads during the 1970s. They had a reputation for being supporters of the right-wing National Front. The Section B evolved from their skinhead beginnings in the 1970s into a Casual firm in the mid-1980s. They have retained their extreme far-right politics and have strong links with the BNP as well as the firms from Hearts and Rangers.

JOHN O'KANE

Falkirk – Falkirk Bairns Inc (Fear FBI)

I have to credit the FBI with having the biggest firm
at the Scotland–England match in Glasgow for the
first leg of the play-off in 1999 for qualification to
the European Championships in 2000. The Falkirk
mob also surprised the CSC on the way to the
Scottish Cup semi-final at Ibrox in 1995. A small
group of the CSC boarded an underground train at
St Enoch Square in Glasgow, unaware that the
Falkirk firm were already on board. A scuffle broke
out in which CS gas was sprayed into the carriage of
the train creating a lot of panic. The train emptied as
the small group of Celtic made a hurried exit to
avoid being arrested. The Falkirk Crew ran out of
the station behind the CSC lads catching one of our
boys on the escalator where he received a bit of a bad
kicking. Prior to that incident, the CSC had travelled
regularly to Falkirk without experiencing any
difficulties from the FBI, who we would turn over
with alarming ease.

Kilmarnock

In my 20 years as a football hooligan, I can't recall ever
being involved in a battle against the Kilmarnock firm.
I am not even sure what the hooligan element of the
Rugby Park club calls themselves. However, I have met
a couple of their main lads and, by all accounts, they
have a tidy but small firm.

Partick Thistle – North Glasgow Express (NGE)

I have never really experienced any memorable encounters with the NGE. Back in the late 1980s, we would occasionally come across the NGE who, more often than not, were little more than a group of ICF lads from the postal area of Glasgow. I have since learned that the NGE established a respected Crew within the lower leagues of Scottish football with a firm numbering between 30 and 50 lads who were strictly Thistle and not Rangers.

Other firms associated with clubs in the lower leagues are St Johnstone's Fair City Firm (FCF) and Mainline Baby Squad (MBS), and Dunfermline's Canegle Soccer Services (CSS). There are also firms connected to the likes of Morton, Ayr United, Clyde, Queen of the South, Arbroath, Raith Rovers and Hamilton Academicals.

I admit that I don't know very much about any of these firms, although I could have obtained more information from the internet. However, as I explained elsewhere, I detest the 'Internet Casuals' and wouldn't want to waste my time by sitting in front of a computer and exchanging messages in an abbreviated text that is alien to me. I therefore would like to offer my sincere apologies to any firms that I have failed to mention or whose name has been included incorrectly.

I would stress that the assessments that I have given regarding the major firms are based solely on my own experiences and information received from very reliable sources. I accept that some hooligans will disagree with my assessments and will hold an opinion that may contradict my version of events. That is their prerogative and they are entitled to disagree if they choose. I would like to add that I have attempted to be objective and give an honest portrayal of each firm without exaggeration or prejudice. Hearts excepted!